KAMALA DAS THE INDIAN MONROE

Feminist Perspective

KAMALA DAS
THE INDIAN MONROE
Feminist Perspective

Hongsha Phomrong

ADHYAYAN

ADHYAYAN PUBLISHERS & DISTRIBUTORS
NEW DELHI (INDIA)

Published by
ADHYAYAN PUBLISHERS & DISTRIBUTORS
4378/4B, 105, J.M.D. House, Murari Lal Street
Ansari Road Darya Ganj, New Delhi - 110002
Ph.: 011-23263018, 011-23277156, Fax: 011-23280028
Email: adhyayanpublishers@yahoo.com

Kamala Das The Indian Monroe Feminist Perspective

Edition 2010
ISBN 978-81-8435-227-6

Printed in India

Published by Harish Chandra Yadav for Adhyayan Publishers & Distributors, Laser Typeseting at A.V. Rao and Printed at Tarun Offset Printers, Delhi

Preface

In the hunt for the accumulation of experience, I came across the term 'feminism' which gave me a strong impetus for research works; and, thus I started manoeuvring upon it.

The domain of my findings includes renown feminists such as Lucretia Moth, Martha C. Wright, and Mary Ann Mcclintock associated with the Seneca Falls Convention of the 1830s and 1840s. This was followed by the ever first joint venture of Susan B. Anthony and Elizabeth Cady Stanton, who for the next 50 years were in the forefront of the fight for equality for women in the United States.

A Vindication of the Rights of Women (1792) of Mary Wollstonecraft Godwin of Britain cannot be denied when it comes to the assessment of the feminist movement. Her writing ushered further awakening on the European continent of the rights of women and eventually spread throughout the length and breadth of the world.

Impulse in me then, made me take the work forward to pruning it down to the Indian context with special focus on the works of Kamala Das; because this woman stands unique to the Indian ethos and tastes. Her bold confessions and revelations have taken the entire Indian society by storm and leave its denizens flabbergasted. It is through the paramount force exerted by her person that I have chosen to venturising more about this woman.

In my endeavour and finding, my guide, Dr. Kh. Kunjo Singh, Professor in the Department of English, Former Head, Manipur University, has been a constant inspirer and encourager to me. It is through his guidance and undaunted efforts that I could go forward to the process of research works and making it a reality.

I also thank my younger brother H. Koyaingam for his never-failing assistance in all the minor as well as major printing works of the book. He has been a source of help to me even at the time of odd durance.

My special thanks also go to my dear mother H. Donkhamran for her unceasing prayer support and inspiration and my sister H. Roumundar alias Kh. Leevish for her consistent motivation.

Intellectual support comes from my missus L. Pousheru, Lecturer, Mt. Everest College, Dept. of Chemistry, Senapati and she has also been a source of companion and support throughout the research works.

I must also express my gratitude for the help and support to Dr. V. Alexander Pao, Principal, Mt. Everest College, Senapati and all those friends and well-wishers who supported me during the research work.

Hongsha Phomrong

Contents

1

Introduction

The open and bold expression of Kamala Das (1934-2009) makes her find a niche amongst the literary artists of India. She became the talk of the town when she published her autobiography, *My Story*[1] in the mid-70s at the age of 42 during her serious illness of heart disease. It is also equally interesting to note that this artist professes an honest disclosure of feminity as far as women's issues are concerned.

Kamala Das may be called the Indian Monroe just as Marilyn Monroe (1926-62) is known as the "Goddess of Sex" in Hollywood. It is because Kamala Das' writing titillates and has its leanings on seduction unambiguously. Look at how she arouses the reading-public with an air of exotica as found in her poem, Introduction:

> ....when
> I ask for love, not knowing what else to ask
> For, he drew a youth of sixteen into the
> Bedroom and closed the door. He did not beat me
> But my sad woman-body felt so beaten.
> The weight of my breasts and womb crushed me.
>
> *(Summer in Calcutta, P. 59)*

The above expression is a real masterpiece. It is superb and classic in tone. The reader feels a chill down the spine in an amorous way as it generates excitement and leaves him yearn for sex.

Never before had any woman in India dared to describe so distinctly about the physicality or longing of a woman as Kamala Das.

Her revelation has made the whole Indian society dazed and awesome. It is because of her forceful expression of the problems of women by citing her own story that she came to be accepted as the most daring and controversial poet.

The mention of 'sex' as a word was a taboo to the Nair families. But, to the amazement of her relatives and everyone, she freely mentions it and breaks the traditional canons only to add to the uniqueness of the kind of personality she possesses.

This woman shows her true selfhood successfully by portraying her true identity at the cost of discarding conventional beliefs and practices. She exposes herself by emptying all her feelings and secrecies. In doing so, she also gives vent to her unceasing search for genuine love and experimentation which she thinks must be explored to the fullest extent. She has not only made her personality bare but also has contributed, a sizeable magnitude, to the growth of Indian poetry in English. She will be remembered more as a poet though she has made equal effort in the realm of fiction writing too.

When her autobiography, *My Story* was first published in 1976 raising a lot of hue and cry, some of her relatives were not happy at all. The very publication had rather invited hostile attitude from them. Nonetheless, the pain and anger imbibed to her kith and kin by penning her autobiography has become responsible in boosting her up to a stage of colossal cognizance.

Kamala Das was born at Punnayurkulum in the southern part of Malabar in 1934 as the daughter of V.M. Nair, and Balamani Amma, the Malayalam poetess. She got her education from the Convent School, Calcutta, but could not receive higher education due to her early marriage to K. Madhava Das at the tender age of fifteen. She is known mainly for her collections of poems published in three volumes : *Summer in Calcutta,*[2] *The Descendants,*[3] and *The Old Playhouse and Other Poems.*[4]

Her autobiography, *My Story* is an unprecedented piece of literary work as far as women's writings in India are concerned. This is the reason why the attention of the whole world was attracted and the publication got translated into not less than fourteen different languages of the world. She is a bilingual writer; and her short stories are very popular in Malayalam. Her works in Malayalam include more than fourteen books and the majority of them are collections of short stories. She has won the Poetry Award of the Asian PEN Anthology in 1964, and the Kerala Sahitya Akademi Award 1969 for Cold and a collection of short stories in Malayalam.

The publication of *Summer in Calcutta* has given a different shape to Indo-Anglian poetry. Its coming into being has revolutionized the attitudes, especially of the women-folk. Women writers, for the first time, began to realize the indispensable need to unravel the deep-felt emotions and secrecies without inhibition as was found expressed in the works of Kamala Das. Her launching of the book was also at a time when India was experiencing a status free from colonial powers. Earlier poets had looked at the Holy Books or Historical characters for their themes, while she looked into her own self. Her writings are tinged with the spirit to liberate herself from any cultural or patriarchal dominance established by tradition. She, therefore, writes with the spirit of the Renaissance. Despite the constant male domination which she experienced after her early marriage at fifteen, she desired for freedom and her wish to free herself from the dull routines of domesticity and lust – is voiced in the following lines:

> I shall someday leave, leave the cocoon
> You build around me with the morning tea,
> Love words flung from doorway and of course,
> Your tired lust. I shall someday take
> Wings, fly around, as often petals
> Do when free in air, and your dear ones,
> Just the sad remnant of a root, on double-beds
> And grieve.
>
> ('I Shall Someday', *Summer in Calcutta*, p. 52)

She displays the capacity to determine her own destiny in the overwhelmingly patriarchal framework, and this is one of the essential tenets of all types of feminism – both liberal and radical. Her writings constitute both an act of protest and self-determination. Though her creative writing did generate hostility among the relatives, and sometimes even among friends, she went on it doggedly sustained by the feeling that it was through her writing that she could achieve her true being. She exercises in this a free and moral choice and faces the consequences of this choice which again is an important feminist principle. No doubt, she felt betrayed, disappointed, sad and lonely at her situation, but she did not get bogged down. Her love was like alms looking for a begging bowl that sought for a receptacle. She did not find enough love in her husband's house and this is implicitly shown by the following lines:

> . . . I who have lost my way
> And beg now at stranger's door to
> Receive love at least in small change?[5]

Kamala Das' search for ideal love and the resultant disappointment seem to involve the psychological phenomenon of 'the animus' struggling to project the masculine imprint as interpreted by Jung. The attempt to seek in every lover the perfection of masculine being is destined to end in failure because of the impossibility of realizing the ideal in human form. The poet reveals this awareness in:

> . . . I met a man, loved him call
> Him not by any name, he is everyman
> Who wants a woman, just as I am every
> Woman who seeks love.[6]

The very first collection of her poems has established her as a very different kind of Indian – English woman poet, specially from the earlier generation poets like Toru Dutt or Sarojini Naidu. Her fierce individuality challenging the cultural and traditional systems is shown by the following lines:

> I wore a shirt and my
> Brother's trousers, cut my hair short and ignored

My womanliness. Dress in sarees, be girl,
Be wife, they said.[7]

It was something the Indian readers did not use but against which they could not protest. In a male-dominated world, the earlier women poets had acquiesced with the situation and had rarely felt the subdued position they had been allotted. Whatever may be the standing of Kamala Das as a poet – and hers is certainly high enough to be among the leading poets of today, in spite of her repetitive themes – credit should solely go to her for rebelling so gloriously against the unjust domination of the so-called *Stronger Sex.*

The poetry of Kamala Das has a special force and appeal that ring deep to the reader's sensibility. The force is primarily because of the honesty and candour with which she asserts her right to exist as an individual with a distinctive identity. She tries to be on her authentic self even if this involves breaking the moulds of traditional ethics and propriety. Her poetry voices, a vehement protest against the senseless restrictions which compel a sensitive and intelligent woman, to lead a vapid kind of existence broadly indicated by her in *the Introduction:*

Be embroiderer, be cook
Be a quarreller with servants, fit in, oh
Belong, cried the categorizer.[8]

Kamala Das refused to fit into any scheme devised by the categorizers. The frank and confessional quality of her poetry is her main strength, though in the absence of a mature self-restraint we can also notice in it a dash of callous exhibitionism, particularly when she has to flaunt her flamboyant 'lust' in order to retrieve her undermined dignity.

The bitter irony and anguish of a woman who finds herself tied down to a meaningless routine of household activities can be noticed in many of Kamala Das' poems.

One can see how she struggles to assert her individuality and her own existence in all her poems. She is often grouped under the group of confessional poets. She has succeeded in going into the subconscious needs, desires and aspirations of the feminine mind. In this regard, Anisur Rahaman comments:

> As a poet, she implores her psychic Geography with an exceptional female energy and achieves the capability to express her inimitable vision through the technique of sincerity. Of all the women poets of the present in India, Das projects herself as a fervent feminist poetic voice always exacting the naturalistic, freedom and choices. Her poetry contributes for the most needful awakening of woman as a living entity in being – in – the world.[9]

The modern Indian English poetry with all its aggressiveness finds boldness and culmination in the works of Kamala Das. No other feminist poets in India could achieve the absolute rebellious dimensions of Kamala Das in their poetry. In fact, she makes a poetic revolt by making introspective pondering upon the unfortunate state of existence of Indian women. From the beginning, she demonstrates a continuity of theme and expression concerning her feminist ideals. Kamala Das speaks out her heart both as a woman and as a poet. She struggles to cope with problems and dilemmas. She does not attempt to intellectualise rather she makes a discovery of human existence and narrates her experiences vividly and passionately. She tries to reject masks and roles; and refuses to accept the limitation of her biology too.

When there is no sense of meaningful participation in the social life and the individual is condemned to lead a purposeless existence with no challenging responsibilities to shoulder, she is likely to be haunted by a sense of hollowness and futility. Kamala Das' poetry, as has been mentioned earlier, does have an authenticity and force to the extent that she honestly brings out the triviality and shallowness of the life she has been pushed into to live as a middle class woman. Nonetheless, it is also to observe that the positive human substance of the experiences of such an individual is bound to remain limited so long as he does not boldly repudiate the senseless curbs imposed on him by the situation. Kamala Das does give expression to the restlessness and irritation of a person who has been shut off from the larger currents of social life, but we also notice in her poems a timid attempt to assuage her bitterness by an easy Arnoldian recipe of personal fidelity and intensities of love-experience. In her candid moods Kamala Das admits that love as a tonic is sadly inadequate so long as the individual's role in the social environ does not alter.

Readers will not fail to see to the fact that Kamala Das' poems are tinged with the elements of both the external and internal worlds, and her response to the external world is sharper in particular than her inner restlessness.

Her husband Mr. Das, an official in the Reserve Bank of India, Bombay was an experienced man in sex especially with his maid servants. His contact with his wife was, therefore, usually cruel and brutal. He talked with a tone of boastfulness for his acquaintanceship with the type of women who were nymphomaniacal and sluttish. The attitude of the husband made Kamala Das frustrated and disappointed and as a result, she grew revengeful towards him, and reacted in a non-traditional fashion in love-making, offering herself to any handsome or resourceful man whom she came across, and forgave even her rapists. Her husband had no soothing words for her, no time to spare for her and was ever busy sorting out his files and affixing his signature on them. The traditional duties of a Hindu wife were to offer respect towards her husband; she was expected to discharge her duties well and to look to the needs and comforts of her husband.

This eroded her own distinct personality and dwarfed her forever, as she makes clear in the poem, *The Old Playhouse*:

> ... You called me wife,
>
> I was taught to break saccharine into your tea and
>
> To offer at the right moment the vitamins. Cowering
> Beneath your monstrous ego I ate the magic loaf and
> Became a dwarf. I lost my will and reason, to all your
> Questions I mumbled incoherent replies.[10]

This is actually a strong protest against a hollow marital

bond which she cannot untie. In India where marriage and love go hand in hand, it is most unfortunate that such a sensitive woman as Kamala Das is tied to a stake where she cannot fly. Such occurrences are not uncommon in the land of Gandhi and Nehru, turning many a woman tragic and gloomy in their attitudes towards life. Kamala Das has made repeated protests against this sort of situation in her poetry.

The parental home of Kamala Das was influenced by the movement of Gandhiji. They wore *khadi* clothes, spun *khadi* yarn, especially her grandmother, to whom this girl was deeply attached in her early age and whom she remembered so sweetly in her later life. Mahatma's photos hung in every room. Even the servants felt his presence in the house and began wearing *khaddar*. The Nalapat House which she called her ancestral home, consisted of seven occupants in all, who were her grandmother, her aunt Ammini, her grand-uncle, the poet, her great grandmother, her two sisters, and Mahatmaji.

The life of Kamala Das, as penned by herself in her works, shows a search for man-woman relationship which should guarantee both love and security to a woman. She lives with her husband and looks after her three children who are all sons.

When she speaks of love outside marriage, she does not advocate for the kind of infidelity women should possess nor does she insist to commit adultery; she simply has the curiosity to explore love to the utmost possible level. And it is also important to note that she gives a mythical framework to her search for genuine love and identifies it with the Radha-Krishna myth or with the Mira-Krishna relationship. There are several poems on the Lord Krishna in her volumes, supported by references to this Lord in her prose writings especially *My Story* and *Alphabet of Lust.*[11]

The period from 1968 to 1973 seems to have pushed Kamala Das to a situation giving less poetic power and fecundity. She remained more prosaic during these few years. Her prose works written after *The Descendants*[12] are almost exclusively autobiographical. Frigidity and the "Sepia-tainted Photograph" clearly show her personal experiences and with the subject of love and emotional discontentment in an empty married life. Though her prose writings are controversial, her essays like "I Studied All Men", "What Women Expect Out of Marriage and What They Get", "Why Not More Than One Husband?" and "I Have Lived Beautifully" tend to consolidate her image in public as feminine, forthright, unconventional and yet honest.

Kamala Das caricatures the feminine role to emphasise the plight of being a woman in this world. Her quest for self-knowledge only leads her to the painful realization and she compares herself to an Old Playhouse with all its lights put out. The conflict between passivity and rebellion against the male oriented universe is a theme which preoccupies her most.

Women in the present world seem to search for some kind of identity amidst all the existing problems trying to suppress them. The search for feminist identity has, therefore, become an interesting topic in the realm of research. Under the patriarchal structure, women's manner, ideas and their very souls are modified by the constant pressure of masculine standards. "Economically", quotes Juliet Mitchell, "women are the most highly exploited group; they are also the most physically determined as inferior. This is of course, their position within each race or class. But as a sex, despite national, racial or class differences, they share the overall inferiorization which is total." But with the rise of feminism, women began to discern and discover values of life and rhythms of vitality of their own, without submitting to their criticism of any task-master. For the first time, they had an opportunity to be themselves. Therefore, despite the variation in the biological set-up women must be given an avenue to stand upon and be treated at par with menfolk. In the light of the interpretations and definitions of feminism made above, the writings of Kamala Das are interpreted and investigated in the forthcoming paragraphs.

Kamala Das is a great writer, who tries to create an identity of her own self by breaking down the existing social power structures and create a place for herself in the world of masculine hierarchies. As a woman writer, she could thereby assert her emotion boldly; she writes with a force to alter her existing marginalized position and accepts her rightful role as a significant part of the society. By accepting the self, she could challenge the accepted notions of the female and re-draft a general opinion on the feminine mystique.

In her book, *My Story,* she successfully shows her true selfhood and insists on being herself in the midst of all kinds of pressures, mounted on her by the embedded patriarchal values. She discards altogether, the weakening and constricting conventional taboos which she thinks deteriorate against her essential self and thus breaks open her own cocoon and comes out from it to have a better glimpse of the world around her. The would-be-poet in her is already evident when she says:

> I was very sentimental. I wrote sad poems about dolls who lost their heads and had to remain headless forever. Each poem of mine made me cry.[13]

Kamala Das' autobiography, *My Story,* clearly shows how her urge for identity and liberation finds its fruition and fulfilment in her creative writing. On her emergence as a poet by overcoming her domestic self, she is also compelled to play a role of duality basing on the monotonous enslaved wife and mother. Her such condition is explained by Raji Narasimhan in the following words:

> The heroine of My Story is a semi-educated girl, rudely pushed into marriage, into premature sexual experience, to be left floundering in the quick and of repeated pregnancies and childbirths. This doomed girl overcomes her destiny. There is a heroism about this effort in an earlier age which gives a period weight to the book. It also makes one overlook its mixture of good and bad prose, and its emotional kite-flying.[14]

The ever struggling self in Kamala Das which is desperate for release and fulfilment makes her tone of confession thrilling and enchanting. Her quest for identity often occurs as a theme in several of her poems. She is always on the track to discover her true self. For example, *The Old Playhouse* describes that love aims at achieving an insight into one's own being, not into another's; its essence lies in the realization of one's own self, and not in the loss of one's freedom. Her situation to gain more experiences of life and her own selfhood is seen in the following lines:

> It was not to gather knowledge of yet another
> man that I came to you but to learn what I was,
> and by learning, to learn to grow, ... For, Love
> is narcissus at the water's edge, haunted By its
> lonely face, and yet it must seek at Last and end,
> a pure, a total freedom, it must Will the mirrors
> to shatter and the kind might
> To erase the water.[15]

Kamala Das becomes the mouthpiece for exposing the inherent right of every woman to protest and revolt against all those forces in society which conspire to hinder the development of her personality. She presents a fine and relevant example of being a woman by delineating her own trials and tribulations. We find in her the confronting and overcoming nature of the contrasts a woman faces and a woman who seeks self-awareness and self-fulfilment. And this conception is one of the important aspects of all feminist theories. Unfortunately, the scholars have overlooked or ignored such aspects of her creative personality which are inconvenient to them. A slightly more discreet perusal of this huge scholarship reveals that her love poetry has been misread strategically in fragments to substantiate a thesis which does not hold true in respect of her total output. Conceding that there are several milestones in her evolving sensibility, it is unfair to play up one phase of development to the detriment of the entire creative ambience. The present paper is an attempt at setting the critical perspective right about her appropriation or otherwise of the male space in her poetic oeuvre.

It is true that most Indian women poets treat their theme of love with an intensely personal confessional mode and certain amount of attraction for the feminist views. While their attempt was to explore the 'self' in depth, most of them could scratch only the surface level. However, the poetry of Kamala Das has been hailed as excellent because of the apparent daring imagination, stylistic innovation, richness of energy and moving force. All these qualities spring from her poetic genius; she is a natural poet, not a semi-skilled craftsman trying to construct poetic artefacts. She is an investigator of the impulses, one who is obsessed with the flow of inner experience. Being a natural poet her poems may show different levels of poeticality, depending upon the nature of the spatio-temporal effect on her senses and intellect. The following words of the Soviet poet Bella Akhmadulina throw light upon the way the natural poet would generate poetry:

> After I have lived in some faraway place for about ten days, I suddenly hear a sound . . . the necessary word is found. And then I write and write and for twenty four hours a day without a break until the guiding sound has faded away.[16]

An idea almost similar to the above quotation is also found in the words of Kamala Das when she says:

> I write only at night when I am left alone and every one else is asleep. Then the world suddenly comes to focus, becomes more my own.[17]

The poetry of Kamala Das is spontaneous, straightforward and simple. She paves the way for the reader to approach to the new fields of feelings and emotions in an earnest manner. What she presents before the reader is a synthesis of rare and contrasting thoughts of lonely minds. She perceives the world as one perceives it in a dream. Though she believes that she has not attained the emotional maturity to write sublime poetry, yet, her heart flows in words abounding in sensual rhythms and soulful laments. The experience she concretises is hers and it could also be anybody else's. Kamala

Das has glorified love in her poems. Love to her is a kind of beautiful religion of which sex is an indispensable part. She views that her love is not mere lust; but gives her inclination to her preference for the sexual kind.

We also find in her poetry an alert and inquisitive approach to life. She draws inspiration from the simple, the sad and the gorgeous events in everyday life. The evenings in the old Nalapat house, the silence around the hanging corpse of a maidservant, the frenzied dance of the eunuchs in the scorching Calcutta afternoon, the smell of death in the hospital wards, the Lankan Street, a vigorous but loveless lover, all inspire her to write. And she writes, dipping the sharp end of her imagination in her simple but sensitive, sensual but sad heart, about the mundane and the ethereal; and the reader witnesses the coalescence of various emotions in her published books of verse.

Kamala Das has succeeded in writing delightful poetry by depicting her personal experience as the main base. She has also gained the applause of the people who once showered on her the venom of negative criticism. It is with extreme sincerity that she pictures her quest for identity. Her writings are filled with the song of a heart that longs for sexual satisfaction, the recollection of the purity and playfulness of the childhood, the broken womanhood, the love of the grandmother, the cruelty and hypocrisy of men, the painful realization of failing youth and the approaching old age and the despair of gerontion itself.

Though many critics have pointed out the failures and limitations of Kamala Das, she still finds adequate expression to translate the various vicissitudes of life. She occupies an important position among the poets who constitute the modern tradition of Indian poetry in English. The poetry of the modern writers like Kamala Das is recommendable to the students on the ground that it successfully meets the basic requirements of all good literature. She possesses clarity of thought, intensity of feeling, refinement and subtlety of expression. She is a woman who knows of her own authentic self and as such would not be guilty of any looseness in thought or feeling or in the handling of language.

She increases our awareness of how the dead weight of outworn values can block the emotional and intellectual growth of an individual. Through the images of the night girls with sham obstrusive breasts walking on the streets and beaming the sickly smiles at men, she brings into a vivid focus the sterile and wasted existence of the wrongly adjusted individual on whom a false role has been imposed. Kamala Das has a sharp nose for the sense of smell and she has the honesty to recognize the happenings around her.

"The Dance of the Eunuchs" shows how painful and irrelevant, the life of an ill-adjusted sensitive individual can be in the rotting and decaying society. The atmosphere and the rhythms in the poem conveys the central image of a group of sterile and harassed individuals, overwhelmed by a sense of destitution and helplessness, dancing their strange and unnatural dance:

> Their voices
> Were harsh, their songs melancholy; they sang of
> Lovers dying and of children left unborn . . .
> Some beat their drums; others beat their sorry breasts
> And wailed, and writhed in vacant ecstasy. They
> were thin in limbs and dry; like half-burnt logs from
> Funeral pyres, a drought and a rottenness
> Were in each of them.

(*Summer in Calcutta*, p. 9)

The vacant ecstasy wrought by these figures symbolizes the restless turmoil experienced by the poet herself. She also discusses the general condition of our society in a poem like The Flag in which the intensity of the feeling shown in the poem is not backed by an adequate understanding of the issues involved. She registers from the outside that there is something wrong somewhere but she fails to pierce beneath the surface and cannot understand the lines as follows :

> The
> Rich men dance with one another's wives and
> Eke out a shabby
> Secret ecstasy, and, poor old men lie
> On wet pavements and

> Cough, cough their lungs out. Yet there is whiskey
> On the breath of winds
> And channel Number Five, and the cooking's
> Smell
>
> *Summer in Calcutta*, p. 21

Kamala Das seems to have an audacity and a naivety in the course of the problems of the poor as if she had drawn up a plebiscite with them, and the feeling that she sides with the poor may be seen in the following words taken from her autobiography.

> I have often wondered why the government cannot pass an order that all huge buildings must be let out their basement hall for the homeless during the harsh monsoons and during the winter. Every hotel can be made to spend one-tenth of its daily earnings in feeding the poor. Charity is India's ancient tradition, there is no harm in serving it when the times are hard.
>
> (*My Story*, pp. 200-01)

A close reading of her works tells that she is sometimes haunted by a sense of hollowness and futility since there is no sense of meaningful participation in the social life. She brings out the triviality, vicissitude and shallowness of the life she is destined to live as a woman belonging to the middle class. She gives an expression of the restlessness and the irritation of a person who has been scrapped from the larger currents of social life, but we also notice in her poems a timid attempt to rise above all these lonely experiences.

In her candid moods Kamala Das hunts for true love. She analyses and synthesises the meaning of love; but love cannot be found in the human form. She, therefore, focuses her search for true love to the divine, Lord Krishna.

Whatsoever the case may be, Kamala Das enjoys substantial visibility today as a woman writer and her works are widely read. It is also the responsibility of such a feminist writer to arouse the inactive, lethargic women from their slumber, so that they shed their baseless fears and inhibitions and stand up against the forces which are curbing their progress and freedom. These women should come together and unite themselves to fight against the unjust forces of patriarchy.

Love, respectability and freedom are some of the indispensable passions that go along with life; and, these are the desires which almost every individual runs after. However, they cannot come so easily to a person especially to the womenfolk. Women must work hard for the attainment of these passions. Freedom will afford them a chance to improve their lot. The effort of a handful people will be ineffective, a mass movement is what is required.

The poetry of Kamala Das is based on her undaunted effort to fight against the unjust male hegemony. She is all bent to expose her feelings and emotions without any inhibition and as a result, her poetry is full of eagerness and questions that are rarely answered. They are queries about truth which, at certain situations, seem incongruous and unbearable. Her forceful question on sex, rarely appreciated by her admirers and friends alike, is also seen in the following lines:

When a man is dead, or a women,
We call the corpse not he
Or she but it. Does it
Not mean that we believe
That only the souls have sex and that sex is
Invisible?

("The Doubt", *The Descendants,* p. 22)

Among the contemporary literary figures, Kamala Das occupies a prominent position as a poetess of talent and artistry. She, as a major Indian poetess of English, has attracted international attention by virtue of her bold and uninhibited articulation of feminine urges along with other poets like Gauri Despande, Mamata Kalia, de Souza and others.

Kamala Das is in fact a woman substance. There is always that search for feminist identity in her works. She goes on delving deep into the subconscious mind of a woman by diving into her own self, and unravelling mysteries which were never known to Indian women, or frankly speaking, nobody dared to ravel them in the past, in such a way, in such an orthodox and custom-ridden conservative society.

For centuries together women had suffered mentally and physically under the patriarchal domination. But Kamala Das does not suffer quietly like other women of the past; she tries to fight against all these suppressions.

In the forthcoming chapters, an attempt will be made to show how Kamala Das advocates feminist ideals. Knowing her place and position, she never fails to claim it. The crux of the problem of the so-called man-woman relationship in the established society is that man is born to rule and woman to obey; man, the master and woman the slave, man for the field and woman for the hearth and so on; and such pattern had been followed for many centuries. However, with the rise of Indian women writers in the literary world in or around the 1960s, a new awakening is dawned and the century old mutely followed relationship is now challenged by feminist writers such as Anita Desai, Sashi Despande, Rama Mehta, Jai Nimbkar and poets like Kamala Das, Gauri Despande and others.

The word feminism has aroused great interest amongst people all over the world. A somewhat detailed treatment will be unveiled in the next chapter. When we talk of "feminism" it does not mean that we are talking of equality in the sense that women start dressing up as males or that there should be a reversal of the roles adopted by men and women in the society. Feminism demands, as Kamala Das demands; love, respect, compassion and understanding from the males. If the love of men towards women would stem from devotion, the problems faced by women would be easily solved. Love is a very tender emotion, which comes after much devotion. Love is the essential emotion which binds people together. Everybody craves for such kind of love. Kamala Das also craves for such kind of love but she never got it from her husband.

The search for her identity in a male-dominated society

was a hard task but she'd been able to express her pent-up feelings through her poems. I was somewhat surprised when I first read some of her poems. The way she had exposed man-woman relationship, the sex-intrigues she penned in an unusual manner, the uncontrolled assertion of the various parts of a woman's physique, the freedom she'd exercised in expressing the remorse of her mind, etc., aroused a kind of enthusiasm on the part of the reader. And this is the standing evidence as to why I have chosen the unparalleled artistry found in her especially amongst Indian women writers.

Feminist concern in Indian writing in English, is one of the most striking topics to be discussed upon. The word feminism seems to refer to an intense awareness of identity as a woman, and interest in feminine problems. The subjugation of women is a central fact of history and it is the main cause of all psychological disorders in society. The meaning of the word feminism has so many connotations and has been wrongly interpreted. According to Janet Radcliffe Richards,

> feminism has a strong fundamental case, is intended to mean only that there are excellent reasons for thinking that women suffer from systematic social injustice because of their sex, the proposition is to be regarded as constituting the essence of feminism.[18]

All through history a woman has been in a position to seek fulfilment in her submissive domesticity. Women who were frustrated and disappointed with the aura set for them were considered subversive or neurotic. The same thing happened to Kamala Das. She was not satisfied with the limits set for her and she became restless and neurotic. She thus endorses a scathing attack on male domination and the subjection of women. A number of scholars have also been devoting their time on the study of Indian writings in English. So many books have been published in this regard. Indian writings in English are gaining momentum and popularity day by day. Kamala Das too, as one of the Indian writers writing in English and gaining popularity in a gradual manner, has contributed a lot and her writings have become a context for investigating the term feminism which is broadly discussed in Chapter 2 and minutely, in the remaining chapters.

NOTES AND REFERENCES

1. Kamala Das, *My Story* (New Delhi: Sterling Publishers Pvt. Ltd., 1976). All the subsequent page references are to this edition.

2. Kamala Das, *The Descendants* (Calcutta: Writers Workshop, 1967).

3. Kamala Das, *Summer in Calcutta* (New Delhi: Everest Press, 1965).

4. Kamala Das, *The Old Playhouse and Other Poems* (Madras: Orient Longmans, 1979).

5. Kamala Das, "My Grandmothers House" in *Summer in Calcutta* (New Delhi: Everest Press, 1965), p. 26.

6. *Ibid.*, p. 60.

7. Kamala Das, "An Introduction" in *Summer in Calcutta*, p. 44.

8. *Ibid.*, p. 60.

9. Quoted in Reena Sanasam, "Kamala Das: A Study of Her Quest for Feminist Identity" (Unpublished Ph.D. Thesis submitted to Manipur University), p. 7.

10. Kamala Das "The Old Playhouse and Other Poems" (New Delhi: Orient Longman Pvt. Ltd., 1973), p. 1.

11. Kamala Das, *Alphabet of Lust* (New Delhi: Orient Paperbacks, 1976).

12. Kamala Das, *The Descendants* (New Delhi: Orient Paperbacks, 1976).

13. Kamala Das, *My Story*, p. 8.

14. Raji Narasimhan, "Living Fully in its Poetry: A Reassessment, *The Hindustan Times*, 26 August 1984. Quoted in Reena Sanasam, *Kamala Das : A Quest for Feminist Identity* (unpublished Ph.D. Thesis submitted to Manipur University, 2002).

15. *Summer in Calcutta*, p. 16.

16. V.T. Usha, *Kamala Das: A Critical Spectrum* ed. Rajeshwar Mittapalli and Pier Paolo Piciucco (New Delhi: Atlantic Publishers and Distributors, 2001), p. 18.

17. Atma Ram, *Interviews with Indian English Writers* (Calcutta: Writers Workshop, 1983), p. 81.

18. Sushila Singh, *Feminism Theory, Criticism, Analysis* (New Delhi: Pencraft International. 1977), p. 22.

2

Feminism: Multiple Perspectives

The term "Feminism" may be defined as the movement for the political, social and educational equality of women with men. The movement occurred simultaneously in Great Britain and the United States. It had its roots in the humanism of the eighteenth century and in the "Industrial Revolution", both of which contributed to the emergence of society transisted from a feudal aristocracy to an industrial democracy. Women had been regarded as inferior to men physically and intellectually. Both tradition and theology had ordered their subjection. Women could not in their own names possess any property. They could not engage themselves freely in business, or control the disposal of their children or even of their own persons. Although Mary Astell and others had pleaded earlier for larger opportunities for women, the first great feminist document was Mary Wollstonecraft's *Vindication of the Rights of Women* (1792).[1]

In the French Revolution, women's republican clubs demanded that liberty, equality, and fraternity be applied regardless of sex, but this movement was extinguished for the time being by the Code of Napoleon. In North America, although Abigail Adams and Mercy Otis Warren had pressed George Washington and Thomas Jefferson for the inclusion of women's emancipation in the constitution, the feminist movement really dates from 1848, when Elizabeth Cady Stanton, Lucretia Coffin Mott, and a few others, in a women's convention at Seneca Falls, New York, issued a declaration of independence for women, demanding full legal equality, full educational and commercial opportunities, equal compensation and the right to collect wages, and the right to vote. Led by Elizabeth Cady Stanton and Susan Brownwell Anthony, the movement spread rapidly and soon extended to Europe. Little by little, women's demands for higher education, entrance into all trades and professions, married women's property and other rights, and the right to vote were conceded In the United States after women's suffrage was won in 1920, women were divided on the question of equal standing with men advocated by the National Women's Party *versus* some protective legislation; various forms of protective legislation had been enacted in the nineteenth century e.g., limiting the numbers of hours women could work per week and excluding women from certain high risk occupations. In 1946 the UN Commission on the status of women was established to secure equal political rights, economic rights, and educational opportunities for women throughout the world.

In the 1960s "feminism", or the Women's Liberation movement as it became known, experienced a rebirth, especially in the United States. The National Organisation for Women (NOW), formed in 1966, had over 400 local chapters by the early 1970s. NOW, the National Women's Political Caucus, and other groups pressed for such changes as abortion reform, federally supported child care centres, equal pay for women, the occupational upgrading of women, and generally removing all legal and social barriers to education, political influence and economic power for women.

With the leadership of Bella Abzug, Shirley Chisolm, Betty Friedan, Gloria Steinem, and others, the movement successfully influenced Congress to pass the Equal Rights Amendment Bill in 1972; the Amendment, requiring ratification by 38 states, would bar sex discrimination at the national level.[2]

The analysis of feminist concept tries to understand the material conditions through which gender has been constructed within specific languages and bodies of literature. The strong wave in the 1960s and 1970s helped to theorize a women's discourse. In the 1980s "feminism" concentrated on transforming the individual fields, and in the 1990s began a major role in directing academic focus on the concern of the so-called "otherness", "difference" and questions of marginality. It proved to be the moving force in the advent of culture studies.

The concept of "woman" is the central point in the formation of feminist theory. But as a concept it is radically problematic because it is crowded with the over determinations of male supremacy – invoking in every formulation the limit, contrasting other, or mediated self-reflection of cultural built on the control of women. Recent theorists resist the universalising tendency of cultural feminism and highlight the difference between women and men, in a way that undercuts arguments for the existence of an overarching gendered essence.

Margaret Homans has rightly pointed out that the concept of feminism raises fundamental questions about reading, writing, and the teaching of literature. It operates as an interdisciplinary tool for social and cultural analysis and as a political practice. Feminism has transformed the perception of life and literature. Literary theorists believe that feminist criticism does not denote simply the addition of a new subject matter to an existing system of knowledge. It is but a new area of study by adding "women" to "literature" which helps in exposing the incompleteness of what once seemed universal. Therefore, a rethinking on the whole critical enterprise becomes necessary. As argued by Bell Hooks, in the ultimate analysis, feminism dismantles all systems of domination.

Ever since antiquity, women were not given due importance. They were treated as inferior species and source of objects giving vent to the phallic drives of men. Decision either in the family or community was, therefore, arrived at by male-folks only. This made the responsibility of a woman to be confined within the four walls of a room in terms of child-bearing, domestic chores and the caring of the young. Such assumptions, however, were challenged and their cogency became controversial in the wake of the Feminist Movement in the 1960s. This unprecedented arrival of the so-called Feminist Movement has given rise to such genres as psychology, sociology and psychoanalysis with regard to women.

Virginia Woolf is right in picturing them as organisms that had been under the shadow of the rock three million years and were now timidly crawling into the lights.

Feminism is neither a fad nor a logical extension of the civil rights movement. The inequities against which the feminists protest — legal, social and economic restrictions on the basic rights of women – have existed throughout history and in all civilizations. Naturally the principles of feminism were articulated long ago. Women's liberation seems new only because it follows a bill in feminist activism. When the suffragists won the vote for American women in 1920, many of them thought they had achieved the ultimate victory. In the subsequent years, social pressures continued to restrict women's freedom as effectively as the constitutional barriers had done earlier. A feminine mystique evolved, and sanctified the elements of women's experience that proved paradoxically to be most oppressive. Thus, a reawakening of feminist feelings was dawned with the impact of the 1960s.

In the European society before the French Revolution, feminism was thought of as a phenomenon. Most Anglo-American studies of the women's movement acknowledge some forerunners in the English and French Revolutions and in individual figures such as Anne Hutchinson. But only with Seneca Falls does a continuously developing body of feminist thought seems to emerge. French feminism claims a longer past and identifies Christina de Pisan (1364-1430) as the first to have held modern feminist views. She was the first ever feminist to spark off the four-century-long debate on women which came to be known as "querelles des femmes". John Kelly says:

> If Petrarch can be called the first modern man, then Christina de Pisan, the poet and author who introduced her countrymen Petrarch and Boccaccio, to Parisian culture in the early 1400, is surely the first modern woman.[3]

The term "feminism" was not used by early feminists. Had they given any name to themselves, possibly it would have been something like "defenders" or "advocates" of women. The long line of pro-women writers from Christina de Pisan to Mary Wollstonecraft defines an outlook within which ideas develop, a theory in the original sense of the term, a conceptual vision takes shape.

There were celibate lay women who sought to live in their own communities in the late medieval cities opposing misogyny and male subjection; and to support themselves by their collective works. Thus they tried to escape the two major institutions of male power: the family and the church. This movement, however did not gain social acceptance and the state and the church together succeeded in crushing it.

In the 1630s and 1650s many of the radical English sects supported religious equality for women. In this climate, there were women who effectively liberated themselves from the male clerical authority. They sought to control their own conscience, to preach, and to improve women's educational and economic opportunities. These women, like Anne Hutchinson, were "feminists in action", rather than theorists. They used their ideas to modify or organise social forms in which women might be free of male power and authority over them. Their heirs are the women of the later nineteenth and twentieth-century revolutionary movements. By that time feminist activity had stimulated theoretical reflection. The feminist theory later gave rise to a woman's movement for democratic change. New ideas regarding social reorganisation were afloat in the air. The early feminist theorists had carried on their long and patient intellectual resistance against a removal from action. The struggle was carried on mostly by the female members of distinctive modern and literate class representing the upper reaches of a ranked society. They were the forebearers of what Virginia Woolf called, "the daughters of educated men" – daughters in revolt against the fathers who schooled some of them for a society strictly forbidden to other women.

The feminism of the nineteenth and the early twentieth centuries focussed on the acquisition of a few political rights and liberty for women, such as the right of married women to own property and enter into contracts, the right of defendants to have women on juries, and the crucial right to vote. A campaign lasting for a century ensued and culminated in the winning of the right to vote in England in 1918 and in America in 1920.

But without the significant role played by Mary Wollstonecraft (1750-97) and John Stuart Mill (1806-73) in this crusade, this could not have been possible. Ironically, Mary Wollstonecraft, one of the earliest crusaders for the emancipation of women, is remembered by literary historians as the wife of the philosopher William Godwin and the mother-in-law of the poet Shelley. Her whole life and her works were one long protest against the institutions that denied women any other identity except the one they acquired through men. She knew through bitter experience the hardships women faced and were exposed to simply by virtue of their sex. Influenced by the revolutionary fervour of the time, and by her association with a group of radical writers, artists, and philosophers including William Godwin and Thomas Paine, the author of the *Rights of Men*, she wrote *A Vindication of the Rights of Women*" (1792). This book aroused wide and violent response. Horace Walpole resolved never to read it and attacked the author as a "hyena in petticoats". Other writers also attacked and burlesqued with strong objection to its contaminating influence. Ironically, *A Vindication of the Rights of Women,* which anticipated virtually all the demands of the woman's movement – education, legal representation, the right to vote, the right to property, and admission to professions – was read by very few in the nineteenth century. Hers is an extreme ironic example of the treatment posterity accords to a feminist writer.

Similarly, John Stuart Mill's sympathetic attitude towards feminism was one aspect of his belief that the liberty of the individual is absolutely necessary for the development of the society. In his, "The Subjection of Women" he says:

> that the principle which regulates the existing social relation between the two sexes – the legal sub-

> ordinations of one sex to the other – is wrong in itself, and now one of the chief hindrances to human improvement; and that it ought to be replaced by a principle of perfect equality, admitting no power or privilege on the one side, nor disability on the other.[4]

Mill held the view that women's position is not natural but the result of political oppression by men. His analysis of the effects of this use of power on both men and women is exceptionally persuasive. Yet the crux of the book, and the reason for the hostility it provoked, is its radical criticism of the family. He maintained that the masculine domination of the family was a corrupting influence, making boys selfish and girls abject.

Simone de Beauvoir writes in *The Second Sex*:

> The terms masculine and feminine are used symmetrically only as a matter of form, as on legal papers. In actuality the relation of the two sexes is not quite like that of the two electrical poles, for man represents both the positive and the neutral, as is indicated by the common use of man to designate human beings in general; whereas woman represents only the negative, defined by limiting critic without reciprocity.... A man is in the right in being a man, it is the woman who is in the wrong. It amounts to this: just as for the ancients there was an absolute vertical with reference to which the oblique was defined, so there is an absolute human type, the masculine.[5]

The philosophy that fights against the injustice on women, and aims at placing women in a just perspective is called feminism. The word "feminism", however, must be understood in its broadest sense as referring to an immense awareness of identity as a woman, and interest in feminine problems, the meaning should not be restricted to the advocacy of women's rights alone.

The conservatives view that the differential treatment of women, as a group, is not unjust. They admit that some individual women suffer from hardships. But this suffering is not a part of the systematic social oppression. They rationalize the differences between women's and men's social roles in two ways: (i) that the female role is not inferior to that of the male, (ii) or that the women are inherently better adapted than men to the traditional female sex role. Thus while the former claim advocates a kind of sexual apartheid, the latter postulates an inherent inequality between sexes.

Writers who advance such a view range from Rousseau, through Schopenhaur, Fichte (*The Science of Rights*), Nietzsche (*Thus Spake Zarathustra*), and Freud down in the present time to Steven Golberg with the *Inevitability of Patriarchy* (Jagger 19).

They argue that social differentiation between the sexes is not unjust, since justice not only allows but requires us to treat unequals unequally.

Liberal feminism views liberation for women as the freedom to determine their own social role and to compete with men on terms that are as equal as possible. This tradition has continued in various moderate groups like the (NOW), which agitate for legal reform to improve the status of women.

The classical Marxist feminist opines the oppression of women as historically and currently a direct result of the institution of private property. The solution, therefore, lies with the abolition of that institution. Consequently, feminism must be seen as part of a broader struggle to achieve a communist society. Feminism is one reason for communism. The long-term interests of women are those of the working class.

The Marxists theorize that oppression is the chief characteristic of the fight they are for. They are against the society where a small class of individuals owns the means of production and hence dominate the lives of the majority who are forced to sell their labour power in order to survive. Women have an equal interest with men in eliminating such a class society.

Marxists, moreover, recognised that women suffer special forms of oppression to which men are not subject and hence, in so far as this oppression is rooted in capitalism, women have additional reasons to work for the overthrow of that economic system.

Meanwhile, a recent attempt to create a new conceptual model for understanding many different forms of social oppression in terms of the basic concept of sexual oppression has been formulated by the Radical feminists such as Tigrace Atkinson and Shulamith Firestone. They deny the liberal claim that the basic of women's oppression consists in their lack of political or civil rights. Similarly, they reject the classical Marxist belief that basically women are oppressed because they live in a class society.

The origin of women's subjection, according to them, lies in the fact of the weakness caused by childbearing; and, women become dependent on men for physical survival. The origin of the family, thus, is primarily a biological factor. These radical feminists believe that the physical subjection of women by men was historically the basic form of oppression, prior to the institution of private property and its corollary and class oppression. Consequently, the power relationships that develop within the biological family provide a model for understanding all other types of oppression such as racism and class. Thus, the battle against racism is subsidiary to the more fundamental struggle against sexism. Hence, the radical feminists conclude that women's liberation requires an indispensable biological revolution by adopting new technologies. They talk of achieving this through the development of techniques of artificial reproduction.

The above discourse is a briefing of the various existing theories which the feminists have attached themselves to, accordingly. But feminism as a philosophy of study must be conceded that it envisages profound changes in the traditional social structures such as the family, in the economic role and the power of women, a sane personal relationships leading to a just social order.

To understand and sympathise the sensibility of feminism in its wholistic perspective, it is important to observe that Indian feminism presents an altogether different picturesque scene. Regardless of whether it is based on capitalist or on socialist political ideologies, all the countries of Europe and North America claim equality as one of the core principles of their political philosophies. Beginning with the liberal ideals of Locke or Rousseau, that triggered the French Revolution on to the Declaration of Independence that led to the birth of the American Constitution and the consolidation of the USA as a democratic federation, European and American societies have since the last three or four decades of the eighteenth century loudly asserted equality. However, they have not yielded to the acceptance of women-folk as equals. The long and painful suffragette movements constituted by women, the bitter struggles for the acceptance of the idea of equal pay for equal work, the continuing battles on behalf of women's right to abortion and to the practice of birth control, are some of the visible marks of the gender inequality that has persisted and that women had to fight for in spite of the commitments they were made. Under the circumstances, feminist situation in India poses a dissimilar dispensation. Indian society has always been highly hierarchical. The several hierarchies within the family concerning age, sex, ordinal position, consanguinal and affinal relationships or within the community referring to the caste, lineage, learning, wealth, occupation and relationship with the ruling power have been maintained very strictly. The Indians followed these practices urged and integrated by means of a complex combination of custom, functionality and religious belief.

The oppressiveness and the harshness purported by virtue of all these hierarchies are somewhat appeased by a strong sense of deference to superiors, a sense of mutuality, a series of behavioural codes which bend superiors to fulfil their obligations to their inferiors and, above all, by a philosophy of self-denial, and the cultural emphasis on sublimating the ego.

The situation of women in India is in fact quite miserable

and a great deal needs to be done on their behalf. It is a pity that the Indian statement of their problems is often couched in statements that sound alien and which, therefore, fail to hit the mark. In order to gain massive support for women's cause in the country, it is necessary that Indian feminists understand the Indian context thoroughly and that they phrase their criticism, their arguments and their demands on behalf of women with sensitivity to the Indian aura.

The conceptual bearings of "equality" as a correlate of the concept of individual freedom, is alien to Indian society. It was first introduced into Indian culture through Western education and through the exposure of Western educated Indians to liberalism at the beginning of the nineteenth century. However, this notion of equality did not become operational as a principle to Indian life until the country achieved independence and adopted a democratic system of government some fifty years ago. At that point of time, the Constitution of India granted women political status fully equal to that of men. Thus Indian women did not have to bear the brunt of injustices that women in the West had to suffer because of the continuing gap between political ideals and realities. Nor did they have to suffer the kind of indignities European and American women have had to experience in the course of their efforts to bridge this gap.

Truly speaking, the history of India reveals an almost opposite experience. As Western educated Indians came to be acquainted with European liberalism, they were profusely stimulated to reflect upon their own value system and to examine the inequalities, injustices and oppressions of their own culture. This introspection was a moving force for a strong movement for social reform.

The tenacious struggle of Raja Rammohun Roy for the abolition of *sati* is an indispensable crusade which also marks the beginning of the movement for reform on behalf of women. Launched during the third decade of the nineteenth century, this movement constituted an important landmark in the Indian effort towards the emancipation of women. Several aspects of this movement deserve consideration as features that illustrate the uniqueness of the Indian context and mark the issue of feminism in India as distinctly different from the issue in the west.

Describing the reaction to the feminist movement in India, Suma Chitnis writes:

> The most distinctive feature of this movement is that it was initiated by men. It was only towards the end of the century that women joined the fray. The list of men who championed the cause of women is long . . . Raja Rammohun Roy, Ishwar Chandra Vidyasagar, Keshav Chandra Sen, Malabari, Phule, Agarkar, Ranade, Karve ... to mention but a very few. The record of the reform they undertook to achieve is impressive. It reveals that their efforts spanned action to abolish the practice of sati, the custom of child marriage, the custom of disfiguring widows, the ban on the remarriage of upper caste Hindu widows and a host of other evil practices that affected women. It further reveals that while they concentrated on removing evil practices these men were also actively engaged in advancing the status of women by promoting their education, by obtaining for them legal rights to property, and by requiring the law to take cognizance of their status by providing them with some basic rights in matters such as adoption.[6]

These nineteenth and early twentieth centuries benefactors of women endorse a feature of significance in that they pushed reform on behalf of women in the face of total unwillingness on the part of the British government to interfere with Indian customs. The British, however, were unwilling to interfere with Indian custom for the simple reason that they feared that tampering with tradition would make them unpopular and destabilise their rule. Thus, as rulers, concerned about the stability of their empire in India, they were willing to put aside their liberal values and moral convictions, and to allow their subjects to continue with inhuman practices against women. It was only because of the dogged persistence of their western-educated subjects that they were compelled to yield. The quality of this doggedness is evidenced by the fact that when, towards the end of the century, the interest of the reform movement coincided with that of the nationalist movement for freedom; several of the reformers, who happened also to be committed nationalists, attributed prior to reform. The conflict between the obligation for reformation and the commitment for the struggle for self-rule, thus, was highly significant in shaping the status of women in India at the end of the nineteenth century and the beginning of the twentieth century.

Some of the Indian elites who obtained Western education through the exposure to European morals and philosophy at the beginning of the nineteenth century had a critical implication for Indian thought, mores and culture. The powerful influence of European liberalism on Indians was, as pointed out earlier, to stimulate them to reflect upon their own culture, to question some of the customs and practices that they had earlier accepted with equanimity and to move in the direction of reform. It was this impulse that generated the social reform movement and guided its course. The Indians believed that their British rulers would bring about the reforms and changes required to advance Indian society towards the liberal value system.

However, towards the last three decades of the nineteenth century the Indian outlook regarding the British began to change. Even those who had earlier admired the British were growing to be disillusioned with British rule and sceptical of British intentions after experiencing the timidity for reform of these rulers. The scepticism combined with the growing impact of liberal political ideology generated a desire for political freedom and self-rule. The flame of the ideology for freedom and self-rule perpetually becomes answerable to the rise of feminist movement in India.

The emergence of Gandhi as the national leader in the political arena, called for the people to arm themselves morally and declared that the eradication of untouchability, the acceptance of equality for women, liberation from crippling superstition and fear, and the cultivation of humanism must be the prioritized ideals. He directly declared that equality for women would be one of the central objectives of his political programme.

In addition to the above he did much more while explaining the concept of *ahimsa*, he likened the moral power in a non-violent struggle to the pure and gentle, but firm and tenacious strength which, he emphasised, women continuously display in life. Finally, at the organisational level, he emphasised that nothing less than the total involvement of the entire population in the non-violent struggle for freedom would be adequate, and in this context, he pointed out that it was imperative to involve women in the mass movement. With all the persuasiveness and charisma at his command, he urged women to step out of their homes and join him.

Tracing of the legends, historical records and scriptural texts unveil us the irresistible presence of women. Since time immemorial we find the indispensable partnership of men with women. According to the *Holy Bible* of the Christians, God created a woman also as He created a man. This is seen in the Book of Genesis:

> And the Lord said, "It is not good that man should be alone; I will make him a helper comparable to him."
>
> And the Lord God caused a deep sleep to fall on Adam, and he slept; and He took one of his ribs, and closed up the flesh in its place.
>
> Then the rib which the Lord God had taken from man He made into a woman, and He brought her to the man.[7]

Similarly, the inseparable attachment of man to women is also found in the Hindu religion. The Hindu religion too, carried a highly positive concept of the feminine principle. The female principle complements and completes the male. The polytheistic Hindu pantheon consists of divine couples such as Shiva and Shakti, Purusha and Prakriti, Rama and Sita, etc. Together the male and the female represent the specific power for which they are venerated.

It is significant that the deities of knowledge (Sarasvati)

and wealth (Laksmi) are females. Correspondingly, there is a distinctive place for women in the practice of the Hindu religion. Women, particularly those who are virgins or virtuous wives, are believed to have special spiritual powers. Their prayers, penances or supplications to God are believed to earn grace more readily than the prayers of men. Several of the most important sacrifices conferring to religiosity, ceremonies and rituals can only be performed by a married couple. They cannot be performed by either single man or single woman, widows or widowers.

Now having seen\the inseparable association of men with women, we may hence introspect the emergence of feminism in the Indian context. The authenticity of feminine sensibility and feminine experiences would demand a brief scrutiny of the changing position of women in India. As Indian women poets belong to the Indian feminine poetic tradition, an attempt will have to be made also to trace this tradition in general. Only then will it be possible to work out a tentative history of the development of Indian feminine poetic sensibility as expressed in English.

The study of the Indian feminine psyche evolves a change from the tradition to modernity. Critics have proposed various methods to define these patterns of change. For instance, K.R.S. Iyengar, divides the history of Indian writing in English in three general periods — 1875 to 1900 : the new flowering of the creative Indian genius; 1900 to 1947 : the Gandhian Era, and 1947 onwards : the post-Independence period. Rameshwar Gupta, meanwhile, designates the three phases of Indian poetry in English in particular as the Toru Dutt period (1830 to 1912), the Tagore Period (1912-42), and the Aurobindo Period (1942 onwards). V.K. Gokak, on the other hand, divides this poetry into four phases : (i) The last quarter of the nineteenth century: Romantic and Victorian type, (ii) The first quarter of the twentieth century: Continuation of the Romantic and Victorian type and the new trend of Georgianism, (iii) The second quarter of the twentieth century: Modernist and Symbolist trends. The post-independence poetry does not receive detailed consideration in any of these classifications, although it has assumed, by now, the significance of being a major phase. Hence, the Indian poetry may be divided into four categories to highlight its significance as : (1) The Romantics, (2) The New Romantics, (3) The Moderns, and (4) The New Poets. The first of these categories defines the trend in pre-independence poetry whereas the remaining categories describe the broad trends in the post-Independence poetry.

The Romantics from the first category take cue from the British romantic tradition and they write under the strong influence of the British tones. They include the pre-Independence poets like Toru Dutt, R.C. Dutt, Manmohan Ghose, Sarojini Naidu, Sri Aurobindo and others. The New Romantics are inclined to the kind of romantic idealism, combining mystical belief with the idealistic conception of life and drawing their imagery both from the natural universe as well as from the world of science and technology. Poets like Monika Verma, Mary Erulkar, Indira Devi, Dhanrajgir, P. Lal, Pritish Nandy, etc., fall in this category. Poets like Nissim Ezekiel, A.K. Ramanujan, Roshen Alkazi, Kamala Das, Sujatha Modayil, Keki Daruwalla, Shiv K. Kumar belong to the trend of The Moderns because of their sense of commitment to reality about the self and the environment. Poets of the younger generation writing at present like Mamta Kalia, Suniti Namjoshi, Gauri Despande, Lalitha Venkateshwaran, Arvind Mehrotra, Gieve Patel, Arun Kolatkar, etc. may be regarded as "The New Poets." They are still in search of viable themes and modes of communication but in the meantime, they accept a sense of commitment to reality like their elders. Of course, it must be noted that the trends of Romanticism, New Romanticism and Modernism from the British poetry stand here for the broad patterns of sensibility and expression modified by the peculiarities of the Indian ethos.

Indian feminism would also include the poetry written by foreign women by virtue of their marriage with the Indians also calls for special focus when it comes to the study of English poetry by Indian women. It is true that a non-Indian woman poet may not necessarily respond to Indian life in a specially Indian way. Yet her transplantation into the Indian cultural pattern generates a unique set of tension which becomes relevant to the Indianness of the Indian context. Her association with the two combined cultures gives rise to an identity of duality so that her poetic milieu is forced to seek resolution of its tension in a more urgent, varied and intense manner than Indian feminine sensibility. Such poets inevitably give access to liking the poetry with Indianness in nature, and their poetic identity offers a useful basis of comparison for the analysis of poetic works of Indian women. Their poetry is studied in an independent category of "outsider-insiders" as they are "outsiders" becoming "insiders" through their introductions into the pattern of Indian life.

The above discussion may be then regarded as a tip to the awareness of the readers that the flame of poetic writing is kept burning in the hands of many a meticulous writer from generation to generation and this has again, vouchsafed a series of genres of study such as psychology, sociology and psychoanalysis and different fields followed by the unprecedented arrival of the Feminist Movement in the 1960s.

The assessment or evaluation of feminist criticism has always been being centred with the publication of the book *The Second Sex* by Simon de Beauvoir in view of its providing a seminal critique of the cultural identification of women as the "other", the "Relative", to man as the defining "subject", the "one", the "Absolute", etc. An equally important text is Kate Millet's *Sexual Politics* which centres in the mechanisms that enforce the relation of power in society. She also hurls a scathing disapproval to Freud for the male bias in his psychoanalytic theory besides officially disapproving authors like D.H. Lawrence and Norman Mailer among others for demonstrating the ways to boost up the aggressive phallic selves and to degrade women as submissive sexual objects. Elaine Showalter feels that feminism displays the urgency and excitement of consciousness to religiosity. Feminism thus has become a study of vast magnitude.

The unprecedented theorising and the critical innovations in feminist writings on either side of the Atlantic over the last couple of decades witness that it is not a unitary theory or procedure, rather manifests an amazing variety of critical vantage points including adaptation of psychoanalytic, Marxist and diverse post-structuralist theories. The feminist writers have exhaustively worked to explain the differences between sex and gender, and between masculinity and femininity besides analysing the sexist and patriarchal elements in language. Fully aware of the ideological role of language in doxifying the constructing gender and thereby marginalising the position of women, they have also tried to develop concentric modes of writing to counter phallocentric strategies of representation. Feminists' concern for a "woman's language" and a "canon" of her own is an open attempt to deconstruct the forms of knowledge which according to Jacques Derrida are "structured around a centre." While feminist theory seeks to codify some general propositions, strategy is more subjective and varies from situation to situation and is heavily depending on the artist's individual accomplishments and obsessive preferences.

In so doing Feminism also tries to travel to the innermost recesses of the human mind and situations. It delves deep into the human situations as a cosmonaut explores the limitless universe. Let's look at the following anecdote in Simone de Beauvoir's *The Second Sex* depicting the free arbitrary love-relationship wrought by situations and circumstances:

> A woman of forty, married twenty years and with grown up children, began to feel that she was unappreciated and that she had wasted her life. She took up new activities and, for one thing, went to the mountains for skiing. There she met a man of thirty and became his mistress.[8]

The above lines mirror the kind of love-intrigues which a woman indulges; and there is a tinge of her degraded morality status because she is a married lady. Feminist study crystallises bare the weak points and the strong points in a woman. It passes through the realm of a woman's world by delineating what she does or the improvement to be done for her in matters of her social and political standing which is also not always sans some disillusioned temperaments.

The study of feminism focuses to the struggle for equality of women, an effort to make women become like men. But the struggle for equal rights historically and politically emphasises the value of women as they are. The very argument then rests precisely on the fact that women are already as valuable as men. But in the situation of women's lack of equal rights, this value must be located as difference, not as equality. Women are of equal human value in their own way. When feminism asserts the value of women as women, then it truly and efficiently counters the systematic devaluation of women under patriarchy. Equality and difference are not antithetical. But a discourse of female difference, articulated in isolation, runs the risk of echoing the very patriarchal prejudices against which the champions of equality are struggling.

The very essence of equality evolving out of the study of feminism has undergone drastic change in the light of the new French Feminist theories of difference. Through the process of genesis, a female discourse has been evolved by deliberate valorization of repressed femininity. Personalities from France like Jacques Lacan, Jacques Derrida and Gilles Deleuze have propounded the post-modernist theory for putting the correct perspective of the study of feminism. Now all the different strands can be divided into two: relational and individualist theories. Currently relational feminism is being widely accepted as it avoids all the negativism associated with extremities of the individualist theories. The present-day thought encompasses a moral vision and emerges as a wholistic, anti-militaristic and life affirming philosophy.

Toril Moi has made use of the word "post-feminism" to cover the different configurations of feminism and post-modernism prevailing today. Present-day feminist theorists believe that, strictly speaking, feminism is an impossible position. The agonistic definition of feminism sees it as the struggle against all forms of patriarchal and sexist oppression.

Such an oppositional definition postulates feminism as the necessary resistance to patriarchal power. Logically then the aim of feminism as a theory of emancipation becomes abolition of itself along with its opponent. Clarifying the position of feminism Toril Moi voices the following lines:

> In a non sexist, non-patriarchal society feminism will no longer exist.[9]

It is then clear that to defy the study of feminism would obviously mean the defiance of the existence of society in toto as men and women are two inseparable species on the planet earth.

The upsurge ejected out by feminist thought has brought about the materialization of a Utopian quality. Thomas More's Utopia visualized amongst many things a national system of education extended to men and women alike. More's wanton tendency to siphon off a separate place for women is undeniable in this regard. In his coinage of the word "Utopia", he meant 'nowhere land' or 'no place'. A suggested sense of unreality thus becomes an important component of Utopianism. Feminist thinkers have carefully contemplated over and conceptualized societal structures which guarantee women their rightful place in the scheming of things. To recapitulate the Seneca Falls Convention of June, 1848 and its aftermaths and, wherein a series of conventions were organised under the able leadership of Susan B. Anthony and Elizabeth Cady Stanton, the former addresses one of the gatherings thus:

> Are women persons ? And I hardly believe any of our opponents will have the hardihood to say they are not. Being persons, then, women are citizens and no state has a right to make any law or to enforce any old law That shall abridge their privileges or immunities. Hence, any discrimination against women in the constitutions and laws of the several states is today null and void, as is everyone against negroes.[10]

The above speech by Susan Brownwell Anthony is an ironical remark over the indifferent attitudes of the patriarchal set-up towards women. The concrete form of flesh and blood along with the intellect that they possess is made to be unfelt and unrecognized by the powerful institution of patriarchy bringing the sense of utopianism. This, according to the feminists, must be ruled out. Their existence must be deciphered. There must be a suggested sense of reality that must become an important component of anti-utopianism as an integral part strongly embedded in the societal structure and through which their cognizance be sensed.

One is not born a woman, one becomes one.[11]

Male institution is responsible in shaping and determining the social position of women. They are not born as women. It is the social institutions that thrust them to become what they are. Simone de Beauvoir opines that patriarchal oppression imposes certain social standards of feminity on all biological women in order to prove that these standards for "feminity" are natural. To make women believe that there is such a thing as essence of femaleness, called feminity, serves the interest of patriarchy. Therefore, it is also essential to clarify the confusion of female with feminity. Women are females, but this may not necessarily mean that they will be feminine.

To supplement the discursive course of Utopianism, Hester Eisenstein has used it in a different sense, modifying its fictive and dream-like connotations. For her the utopian element is inherent in the intention of creating a picture of an alternative society. It actually aims at changing the current reality by means of creating a model, or pieces of a model of a society organised along different lines. As the place of women is integrally embedded in social life, any change or disruption means potentially changing or disrupting many things – personal identity and sexual mores, family arrangements, childbearing customs, educational patterns, religious ideology, and political and economic structure. Even if a change is made to this effect in terms of removing all the obstacles to women's full participation in public life and conversely of men's in domestic life, this will simply mean the change of faces retaining the same power structures.

Another view states that the insertion of more women

into public spheres will change the world for the better. This view is based on the concept of women's moral superiority to men. But then the idea is opposed by Hester Eisenstein, Nancy Chodorow and Jane Addams because women, like men, are socially produced beings. They can change and they also can be corrupted by power. The feminist utopia presents a totally different picture where structure of power also transforms. Eisenstein interpretes the term "feminist" or "feminism" as:

> In my understanding of the term "feminist", then, I see an element of visionary, futurist thought. This encompasses a concept of social transformation that, as part of the eventual liberation of women, will change all human relationships for the better. Although centrally about women, their experience, condition, or "estate," in Juliet Mitchell's formulation, feminism is also fundamentally about men, and about social change.[12]

We have seen from the above treatise that various feminists have interpreted the term feminism in many ways. Indian feminists such as Kamala Das, Anita Desai, Eunice de Souza, Shobha De, Shashi Deshpande and Arundhati Roy have also put forth views on feminism from every possible perspective dwelling within the domain of Indian ethos and tastes.

Kamala Das too launches her feminist struggle against the patriarchy ridden Indian society. She pens the problems and the issues of women without inhibition and thereby, creates an altogether new look to the study of gynocriticism in the Indian context. However, feminism as she sees it and having its deep rootedness to the Indian soil may be different from the kind of feminism that the Westerners see it. In one of her interviews with P.P. Raveendran, she stated her stand unequivocally :

> Feminism as the Westerns see it is different from the feminism I sense within myself. Western feminism is an anti-male stance. I can never hate the male because

> I have loved my husband and still love my children, who are sons. And I think from masculine company, I have derived a lot of happiness. So I will never be able to hate them.[13]

It is not that Kamala Das denounces patriarchy totally. It is not that she hates male gender or trying herself to be a misanthrope. She still desires to be with them and finds comforts in their company. But what she wants is an expression of her true selfhood; the yearning for the kind of expression to revealing her feminist identity. In so doing, she tries to liberate from the chains offered by the canons of patriarchy. For a long time, she claims that she has been fettered by the rules and regulations of the society, and thus she thirsts for emancipation. But the emancipation she asserts may again be found with a tinge of distinction as is found in her essay "My Instinct, My Guru" stated below:

> I don't want to be "emancipated", because I have seen so many of them [Women] "totally emancipated". They irritate their husbands. I hear complaints from men, their wives have become "so emancipated" that they dictate and they frighten them, all the men turn into mice. I don't think there is much difference between a man and a woman.[14]

This view on feminism with a slight difference is also the reason why Kamala Das has been exhaustively worked upon as a votary of Feminism by critics belonging to either sexes. In their endeavour to excel and compete one another, some of them have consciously or unconsciously everlooked her creative personality which tantamounts their enthusiasm. However, her autobiography, *My Story* becomes the centre of focus as a text to critics when it comes to the assessment of her worthiness as a poet and writer. K.R. Ramachandran Nair, on the other hand, defies this and makes the following remark:

> Since My story is not a totally factual autobiography, I believe that the critic has to make a judicious use of the information given in it. He should not in a blind of [sic] enthusiasm, pounce upon each juicy bit, as if

> catching the criminal red-handed and pretend to know everything.[15]

Kamala Das' flirtation with other men also becomes answerable to prove her feminist credentials and her flirtatious relations with different men have been frequently cited by critics. In doing so the otherwise perceptive scholars forget that it was a sheer expression of personal vengeance – "My love was like alms looking for a begging bowl" – and to look for a dogmatic ideological stance in it is to miss its import. She could never think of severing relations with her husband and all she did was to be unfaithful to him at least physically. On mental and emotional plane she had complete compatibility with her spouse and all that was possible in a situation like hers was to register her protest that way only. Iqbal Kaur looks at her feminist struggle with "a new kind of morality" in it when he says:

> . . . Kamala Das did display tremendous courage in revolting against the sexual colonialism and providing hope and confidence to young women that they can refuse and reject the victim positions, that they can frustrate the sexist culture's efforts to exploit, passivise and marginalize women.[16]

The type of revolt shown by Kamala Das against the so-called sexual colonialism cannot be termed feminist because it was just toying with love outside the wedlock. One feels surprised to think of the hope and confidence the young women can derive from the example exhibited by Kamala Das where rejection of "the victim position" means clinging on to the colonizer, the patriarchal power. The employment of the modifier "tremendous" by Kaur in the context is rather ironic as it spells doom for domestic peace and harmony inevitably for nothing and such a conduct can be regarded as worse than a conformist's attitude. Rama Rani observes her in the following way:

> With exemplary courage and conviction she has explored the innermost depths of her consciousness in this work [*My Story*]. The unifying principle of her re-collections

> is her overriding feminist concern. She has accepted her womanhood with all its weaknesses and strengths and has thus become a symbol of the liberated new women for her generation.

Besides replacing the modifier "tremendous" by a more laudable adjective "exemplary", P. Lall talks of conviction and one fails to trace even a remotest approximation to this serious word homonymous with commitment in the return of this "prodigal wife" who holds her husband and sons so dearly.

The femininity of Kamala Das is also found expressed in the role of motherhood. She identified herself with her children's well-being; she suffered with them during their illness. She shared their joys, their aspirations and became their playmate. She valued the part she played in her family and the domestic life. The liberal feminists consider woman's role in the social construction, through her contribution to family and domestic life, as important and valuable.

No doubt, Kamala Das felt betrayed, disappointed, sad and lonely at her situation but she rose like a phoenix from the ashes of her emotional ruins, and embarked on a quest for self-fulfilment.

From Mary Wollstonecraft to Betty Friedan and Simone de Beauvoir, an argument has also been made that education for women will free them from constraints and coercion. This was believed to encourage thought and choice and this was not an argument for formal education. The purpose of education may be said to be broadly the creation of self-awareness and the capacity to foreground one's self against constraints imposed by crises and situations. In this sense, too, Kamala Das conforms to the demands of feminism because she constantly educated herself by vast reading. And this exposure to the world of books helped her in understanding her needs, her aspirations and in helping her to exercise her option to achieve happiness and harmony in her otherwise empty life.

Kamala Das presents a fine and relevant example, by delineating her own trials and tribulations, of the possibility of confronting and overcoming the constraints in the way of a woman seeking self-awareness and self-fulfilment; which, in turn, is an offshoot of feminist upsurge.

At best, she can be described as a sensitive poet, transparent and honest in articulating her personal anguish but very much within the ambit of Indian womanhood.

NOTES AND REFERENCES

1. Mary Wollstonecraft, *Vindication of the Rights of Women*, rpt. (London : Penquin Books Ltd., 1985).
2. *Ibid.*
3. Sushila Singh, *Feminism: Theory, Criticism, Analysis* (New Delhi : Pencraft International, 2004), p. 14.
4. John Stuart Mill, The Subjection of Women (Cambridge : The M.I.T. Press, 1989), p. 3.
5. Simone de Beauvoir, *The Second Sex* (New York: Penguin Books, 1984), p. 15.
6. Suma Chitnis, "Feminism : Indian Ethos and Indian Convictions" in *Women in Indian Society* (ed.) Rehana Ghadially (New Delhi, Sage Publications, 2001), p. 84.
7. Genesis, *The Holy Bible*, New King James Version (ed.) Nelson Thomas (Madras: India Bible Literature, 1993), p. 2.
8. Simone de Beauvoir, *The Second Sex*. (New York : Penguin Books, 1984), p. 591.
9. Toril Moi, "Feminism, Post-Modernism, and Style: Recent Feminist Criticism in the United States", *Cultural Critique 9* (Spring 1988), p. 5.
10. Susan B. Anthony, "On Women's Right to Vote" in *World's Greatest Speeches* (ed.) Rohan (New Delhi : Rohan Book Company, 2004), pp. 43-44.
11. *The Second Sex*, p. 295.
12. Hester Eisenstein, *Contemporary Feminist Thought*, (London: Unwin Paperbacks, 1984), p. xiv.

13. "Of Mask and Memories : An Interview with P.P. Raveendran", *Indian Literature.* 155 (May-June), p. 159.
14. Kamala Das, "My Instinct, My Guru", *Indian Literature.* 139 (Sept-Oct., 1990), p. 160.
15. K.R. Ramchandran Nair, *The Poetry of Kamala Das* (New Delhi : Reliance Publishing House, 1993), p. 11.
16. Iqbal Kaur, "Protest Against Sexual Colonialism: Kamala Das' My Story", in Jasbir Jain, (ed.) *Women's Writing,* p. 234.

3

Poetry Collections of Kamala Das

The fame of the Kamala stands unique in the literary world. She is one of the great Indian poets writing in English. Her writing emerges with a peculiar sweeping force whenever she pens her artistic works, or stands on the dais of literary genre, and this peculiarity has attracted a vast magnitude of readers. The unusual characteristics in her is not far to seek since she is frank, bold and controversial.

The boldness that she associates may also be attributed to the choice of the English language as her medium of expression. After all, English language is an alien medium. But she uses it daringly and with confidence. Her affinity for this medium is neither artificial nor superficial. The infatuation that she possesses for this language is explicitly voiced in *An Introduction* shown below :

> . . . I am Indian, very brown born in
> Malabar, I speak three languages, write in
> Two, dream in one. Don't write in English, they said,
> English is not your mother tongue. Why not leave
> Me alone, critics, friends, visiting cousins,
> Everyone of you ? Why not let me speak in
> Any language I like ? The language I speak
> Becomes mine, its distortions, its queerness
> All mine, mine alone. It is half English, half
> Indian, funny perhaps, but it is honest,
> It is as human as I am human, don't

> You see ? It voices my joys, my longings, my
> Hopes, and it is useful to me as cawing
> Is to crows or roaring to the lions, it
> Is human speech, the speech of the mind that is
> Here and not there, a mind that sees and hears and
> Is aware.

The critics who oppose the use of English by Indian writers are of the view that mother-tongue interference will jar the writer's linguistic representation of his imagination and the product would be an intellectual jumble. But the above view may not be applicable in the case of Kamala Das because her use of the medium is as powerful as of any Native speakers. Let us have a look at her major works given below:

Poems of Confessional Tone

The poems of Kamala Das are fused with her love-experience purported by a multi-dimensional phenomenon involving tensions of different kinds. The complex nature of these poems may be properly apprehended by focusing on some of the most important dimensions as defined in terms of her relationship with her husband, the lovers, the grandmother's house and the society as also in terms of her identities as a woman and as a poet. The blatant honesty which she employs as a yardstick gives a quality of uniqueness to her poetic exploration.

Kamala Das' love-experience is ejected from her encounters with her husband which also form the basis for all other rapports that follow at a sequential order with other men in her later life. This love-experience, therefore, provides the most important dimension for her poetic exploration. Her life is interwoven by a juxtaposed situation of trying to find spiritual fulfilment on the one hand, and physical fulfilment on the other. She is often seen being bogged down due to her husband's inability to offer her complete spiritual fulfilment. It is because of the urge for spiritual fulfilment that she tries to flirt and to develop some extra-marital affairs. "She even tries adultery for a short while."[1] All these are found expressed in her poetical oeuvre.

Kamala Das' Poems are found to be concerned with the external as well as the internal worlds, and her response has its inclination to the call of the external world in particular despite her inner restlessness. Mrs. Das' landscape, though it is a part of the inner landscape, can still retain its objective contours. She lets the aesthetic details speak for themselves before they speak for her. These facts are shown by the following study of her poems.

Summer in Calcutta (1965)

This work of poesy opens with the poem, "The Dance of the Eunuchs", which has a tone of irony and temper of the entire volume. There are many poems based on love, but few of which speak of the grandeur belonging to a really exalting love-experience. "The Dance of the Eunuchs" clearly shows, through an external, familiar situation, the poet's strangled desire within. It finds its background on the poet's sudden contact with 'a man who had hurt me when I was fourteen years old', she wanted 'to get him at any cost'. This poem is powerful and courageous and it displays an admirable sense of proportion in the use of imagery and metaphor.

The next poem, 'The Freaks" is a confessional poem where the speaking female voice unburdens the torture of her heart. It paints a rather helpless situation where the man is passive and the woman is burning with desire and thereby becomes helpless. This poem is depicting the lack of human communication and the failure of man-woman relationship. They have lived together for long but like islands unto themselves. While they intend or pretend to make love, their minds never meet, like the East and the West, their minds wander apart. What she grudges most is the man's shallowness, his physical hunger and his lip-love. He could never cross the skin's surface as she clearly shows it in the following lines:

Can't this man with
Nimble finger tips unleash
Nothing more alive than the
Skin's lazy hunger?[2]

Though there is unison of the physiques, the hearts never met. Her heart remained an empty cistern. Her flamboyant lust is a defence-mechanism rather than her inner urge. There is an obvious sense of void created spiritually despite their physical commingling.

Another poem, "In Love", brings the poet face-to-face with an inquiry whether she could call her sexual experience "love'. It radiates with heat and passionate experience. In "Winter" also carries the emblem of the warmness of sexual act, of her soul groping for roots in his body. The identification of love with physical desire is also found in her poem, 'A Relationship'. It was my desire that made him male/and beautiful. The poem "Spoiling the Name" mocks at the significance generally attached to words and, figuratively, to abstractions. A name is an abstraction, and in a woman's case borrowed from someone else, it is a weight and a burden, as all abstractions are. She, therefore, asks:

. . . why should this name, so
Sweet-sounding, enter at all the room
where I go to meet a man
who gives me nothing but himself, who
calls me in his private hours
By no name . . . .[3]

This poem shows Mrs. Das' craftsmanship, but is rhetorical in tone.

Human significance of the restlessness and bewilderment or disappointment and gloom experienced by womenfolk in our society is much greater since the contradictory pressures are present in their life in heightened form. The conscious identity won by these women through education cannot find any meaningful expression in the roles thrust upon them by our society. While men could cultivate the realm of personal relationships as a reserved area for their liberal ideals, women are said to have denied this privilege. There has been hardly any opportunity available to a gifted female who wants to assert her freedom and individuality in the restricted field of man-woman relationships.

Kamala Das, therefore, defies the sensibility mentioned above and her poetry has a special force and ringing appeal for us primarily because of her honesty and candour with which she asserts her rights to exist as an individual with a distinctive identity and to be her genuine self in the midst of all the restrictive pressures even if this involves breaking the moulds of traditional ethics and propriety. Her poetry voices a vehement protest against the senseless restrictions which compel a sensitive and intelligent woman to suffer. She, therefore, raises her voice high which is one of the important tenets of feminism, and is solely to add to the rhapsody of the readers.

The other poem, "An Apology to Goutama" also constructs a dialectical opposition between the ascetic and the sensual, between Gautama and her own man. The opposition is actually between two kinds of eyes, two kinds of voices and two kinds of faces, and rather two modes of living:

> . . . while your arms hold
> My woman-form, his hurting arms
> Hold my very soul. [p. 19]

Thus the poem focuses on this vital contrast for its strength.

A sense of gloominess is also felt in her poem, "*The Fear of the Year*". Meanwhile, "*My Grandmother's House*" has the depiction of another ecstasy of wild despair :

> . . . you cannot believe, darling,
> Can you, that I live in such a house and
> was proud, and loved. . . I who have lost

My way and beg now at stranger's door to
Receive love, at least in small change ? [p. 15]

And in "The Wild Bongainvillea" we are to listen to the poet's poignancy and how she groaned/And moaned, and constantly yearned for a man from/Another town.....' In "The End of Spring", the poet, while waiting for the poet's phone call, sinks into brooding over "the fear of change". And "Too Early the Autumn Sights" also evokes a mood of premature dryness within:

Too early the autumn sights
Have come, too soon my lips
Have lost their hunger, too soon
The singing birds have
Left. [p. 26]

Even in this poem of so conventional a mood, Mrs. Das is able to compress or squeeze out of common images a bit of visionary quality.

"Visitors to the City" is another blatant and passionate etching of a scene composed of "sights and sounds" offered by one morning on Strand Road. "Punishment in Kindergarten" is warm and muffled, and recounts the picnic of the poetess at Victoria Gardens to which she and her classmates were taken, and the incident which followed it. She was all alone near the hedge, while other girls were playing at a distance. The poem demonstrates the poet's potential to smell the flowers as well as the pain of being sighted. It also suggests us about the feminist sense of isolation and her desire to be free.

Mrs. Das presents a feminist movement through her poetry. She discovers the male-hegemony from the inner care of her feminine consciousness. Her search for identity is sex-oriented; and therefore, she delineates her feminist voice through sex-imagery. She is every woman suffering passive pathos in a male hegemonic set-up. Her free mention of sex, her husband's pride of having had contacts with "Sluts and Nymphomaniacs", a pair of beautiful breasts and a faint musk-rat smell in her perspiration: all these confessions deserve applause and appreciation but her statement, "adultery is common with women residing in cities" may not be positively agreed to because this view may hamper the general outlook of women in the society. Our societal structure ought to create enough rooms for those women who would like to preserve the de facto sanctity of husband-wife relationship in sex.

Her poem, "The Siesta" is accompanied by sleepiness 'The sun-lit tank", which brings 'an anonymous peace' to her, or with dreams which "glow pearl-white". But what the mysterious siesta brings to her is neutralized by her supposed inability to meet this alien world which talks of gods and casual sins. However, the poet is concerned more with the vulnerability of the "anonymous peace" of the siesta, its inability to withstand the challenge of the wakeful world rather than with the siesta itself. The display of the potency of this challenge is the poet's oblique commitment to it.

Mrs. Das projects a self-contained mood of sensuous luxury in her title-piece, "Summer in Calcutta". The image of the sun in April in the poem brings a sense of sensuous repletion to the poet. In it we find the warm intoxication which inspires as well as relaxes so that she comes to the statement, 'my worries doze' and

> . . . wee bubbles ring
> My glass, like a bride's
> Nervous smile, and meet
> My lips. Dear, forgive
> This moment's lull in
> Wanting you, the blur
> In memory
>
> [p. 48]

The poet celebrates the mood of temporary triumph over "the defeat of love". It is an Indian poet's creative reaction to the torture of the Indian summer. What distinguishes

Kamala Das' reaction is her unconscious intimacy with this torture.

"With Its Quiet Tongue" expresses the poet's agonized concern with the wretched coldness of heart. Another poem, "My Morning Tree" deals with the familiar theme of desperate longing for fulfilment. Its images are sharp; structure is carefully organized; and mood poignantly objectified. The poet looks forward to the moment of the blossoming of "a sudden flower" in it, though the images like the 'ugly tree' and the 'fleshless limbs' of the tree give no hope of this blossoming. And also reflects her thought of sterility of being a woman. The poem is one of the dark despairs; and the sense of fulfilment which so strongly dominates poems like "Winter", "A Phone Call in the Morning", "Love", Spoiling the Name, "In Love", is here imagined and telescoped but not without involving the cost of an almost brutal irony, for the blossoming may not only come too late but may be the end itself. The "passive" limbs of her desires and passion will flower into a "red, red morning flower" of death.

Like "The Dance of the Eunuchs", "The Testing of the Sirens" has a befitting close. The poet wakes up from a night full of love and lust to a sense of physical loneliness, goes through a drive with another with "a pock-marked face" and, while he is taking her photograph, arises with a keen desire for love which is doomed to remain unfulfilled. Her relationship with either of the lovers is a rootless and detached loyalty of the moment, to the first (of the night) that of the limbs and to the second (with the 'pock-marked face') that of "a smile" which is "such a detached thing". The poem immortalizes the poet's attachment to one of her family friends, a young man of eighteen years, who used to take her out to Victoria Memorial, photographing her against trees and against flowing water, and entertaining her with Hindi film songs.

We have a different category of poems like "The Flag", "Forest Fire", "The Wild Bougainvillea", "Someone Else's Song", and "An Introduction", in her work, Summer in Calcutta. In these poems, there is an attempt to rise above the 'private voice' and depict a larger panorama of experience. The technique is almost always one of assuming a vaster identity as in "Someone Else's Song":

> I am a million, million people
> Talking all at once, with voices
> Raised in clamour, like maids
> At village - wells.
>
> [p. 31]

Or, in "The stranger and I":

> *I've seen you in restaurant, all gay*
> And smoke-filled, on the seat behind
> The pillar, drinking joylessly your
> Sweetened tea, while your left hand
> Softly trembling, crouches on the
> Table clock like a wounded bird . . .
>
> [p. 31]

The tone of Kamala Das' poems depicted in this volume focuses betrayal and presents the poet as a prisoner of her own loneliness and isolation aggravated by complex moods. For instance, the poem, "The Wild Bougainvillea" shows the satisfaction of a peculiar personal need as a necessary distraction from her mood of sadness and loneliness. "It is good world, and packed with distractions". The poem, "An Introduction" is an open and witty piece of self-revelation, and is a beautiful statement of her poetic credo, her attitude to language and experience. The crux of her poem is to have the freedom to be herself. She takes a turning from normal paths to exhibit her true identity. "Fit in", said they. "Belong", cried the categorizers. But she doesn't listen to them. Indeed, she has transformed her alienation from "critics, friends, visiting cousins", who say, "Don't write in English", into a larger and more universal alienation based on the sexual, social and artistic perspective:

> I met a man, loved him, call

> Him not by any name, he is every man
> who wants a woman, just as I am every
> Woman who seeks love.
>
> [p. 60]

It is, however, clear from the above that the poems of Mrs. Das especially in Summer in Calcutta, are charged with a sense of universality which is simply self imposed and not natural for her. The personal moods and feelings in this volume are found to have outweighed the impersonal ones, for sustained universality is not within the poet's reach. She is found to be in her own world and her world is to denounce patriarchal hegemony.

The Descendants (1967): Poems of Sensuality

The second poetic collection of Kamala Das entitled *The Descendants* (1967) is composed of twenty-three poems in all. All these poems are the manifestation of her favourite theme of sexual love. This treatment of sex brings about the bearings of carnal urge in a woman. The question of death is also foremost in this collection. It is, by and large, bitterly death-conscious, perhaps death-obsessed. Some of these poems like the "Invitation", "Composition", and "The Descendants" seem to be solemnised by compassion or humility under a false impression. The reality is that there seems to be a yearning for the pseudo-metaphysical poise and the inability to reckon with emotional defeat and frustration, with a sense of nothingness:

> To be frank,
> I have failed.
> I feel my age and my
> Uselessness.[4]

The poetess is actually rhapsodized by a sense of the smouldering "secret" and "isolation" that 'I am so alone', and that life is a colourless design of crumbling patterns, as we find in her poem, "A Request" which is shown in the following:

When I die
Do not throw the meat and bone away
But pile them up
And
Let them tell
By their smell
What life was worth
On this earth
what love was worth
In the end.

[p. 11]

The above-passage delineates the insignificance and meaninglessness of the poetess' life. The situations she has been thrust upon and the sterility she experiences is being conveyed with a sense of sourness and bitterness. Her poems like "Shut Out That Moon" and "Neutral Tones" are examples of discontentment. The defiance of all positives in life reminds us of the poetical tone which Thomas Hardy employs.

The title poem, "The Descendants", frontiers on nihilism which moves the poet in a direction opposite to the faith in the essential continuity of life suggested by "Death Brings No Loss" (Summer in Calcutta). This poem ends with a ring of finality: 'We are not going to be redeemed, or made new'.

We find weak passages and the lack of dramatic cohesion in another poem, "The Suicide". It is written as a conversation between the poet and the sea. The thematic content of this poem is found to be based on the poet's contemplated or suggested suicide, but the poem finally defies it through a rejuvenated sense of life. The body and the soul, according to her, are inseparable, she cannot choose between a physical death and a spiritual death. For her, the sea is the source of a constant distraction, a nagging threat, and invites her to negation:

The sea is garrulous today. Come in,
Come in. What do you lose by dying, and
Besides, your losses are my gains.[5]

This poem offers her dissolution with a tinge of seduction. The vastless sea may also suggest the insatiable desire in a woman.

Another poem, "A Request" is pregnant with the sense of 'death' which also finds a parallelism through 'Dear night, be my tomb' of "Substitute" and merge into the unredeemed darkness of our own fate, of the wounds and the cross, of the fire and 'the hungry earth' of "The Descendants" which would devour us in the end.

In "The Invitation", we witness the duality of death – while the sea offers one kind of death, a complete negation, her lover whom she can't disobey offers another, metaphorical death i.e. the feeling of 'lying on a funeral pyre or with a burning forehead'. The dictum she employs suggests a state of delirium and the feeling of torture that seems to accompany her more recent treatment of sexual love. In it, we find that she rejects the way of the sea and prefers to shrink or grow in her own way. Although the man has gone for good, the poet is still haunted by the memory of her past experience and is warmed in doing so. She cannot forget the self-contained intensity of the moment of sexual love :

All through that summer's afternoons we lay
On beds, our limbs inert, cells expanding
Into throbbing suns. The heat had
Blotted our thoughts. . . .[6]

The above lines show an explicitly suffusing organic warmth and vivify the pervading heat of summer days.

The poem "Ferns" arrests sexual love in an image of self-mocking and self-devouring intensity which suggests that perhaps there is a sense in which her glorification of physical love carries with it an element of disenchantment.

The poem "Convicts", is an evidence of physical love in the elemental terms of physical labour and heat, and a physical experience shown below :

That was the only kind of love,

This hacking at each other's parts
Like convicts hacking, breaking clods
At noon. We were earth under hot
Sun. There was a burning in our
Veins and the cool mountain nights did
Nothing to lessen heat. When he
And I were one, we were neither
Male nor female.[7]

This is indeed, a sensuous poetic passage hurling amorous implication to the readers.

"Substitute" is a poem which hovers amidst poignancy and truculence. In it, we find the need to conform to the convention of a hypocritical society and makes one's feeling of emptiness all the more painful. The poem is full of pathos and is found to be ironical in its meditative refrain:

It will be all right If I join clubs
And flirt a little over telephone.
It will be all right, it will be all right.
I am the type that endures,
It will be all right, it will be all right
It will be all right between the world and me.[8]

This refrain experiences an abrupt intrusion of the image of crows over the market square waving violently but aimlessly in the sky 'with raucous cries' breaks the spell only to prepare the ground for the suggestion of the lack of 'mental contact' between the man and woman in "Our bodies after love-making". The tone of this poem is in the manner of Prufrock's 'Love Song'. The pursuit of love in it is merely mechanical without any meaning.

Another poem concentrating on sexual love is "The Looking Glass" which is shown below:

. . . notice the perfection
of his limbs, his eyes reddening under
Shower, the shy walk across the bathroom floor,

Dropping towels, and the jerky way he
urinates. All the fond details that make
Him male and your only man. Gift him all,
Gift him what makes you woman, the scent of
Long hair, the musk of sweat between the breasts,
The warm shock of menstrual blood, and all your
Endless female hungers.[9]

The tone of the above lines shows close attachment and a ringing indulgence.

The poem, "Captive" presents us the love of Kamala Das as 'an empty gift', 'a gilded empty container' and herself as the prisoner of the womb's blinded hunger, 'the muted whisper at the core'. Its tonic significance is found to be ambiguous and the theme of sexual love receives greater relevance from the charms of creation, and of childbirth. The same treatment of theme finds expression also in her "Jaisurya", which amalgamates the narrative and the meditative and which also details the whole gamut of feelings preceding and following the birth of a son. It brings together light and darkness, and fire and water, to weave a pattern of feeling which holds itself up with the joy of creation. It is noteworthy that meaningful things happen to the poetess at or around noon time under the virgin whiteness of the sun. There was a day of separation from the child which is substantiated by the line 'Separated from darkness that was mine'.

The newly born child is shown with a placement of 'war', 'bloodshed and despair' in "The White Flowers". The earnest prayer wishing her son a long life in the face of the outer threat of violence and death is strengthened by the contrast between the white flowers (symbolizing peace, long life) and the red (symbolizing for blood, mortality, anarchy) of the cherry wine, the rose. In it, we also witness the gesture of heroism as is shown below :

Today some of us will rise and sing of love.
In voices never as sweet before, for love like life
Is sweetest just before its end.[10]

But the glasses are found to be "cold like a dead man's palm" added by the sense of horror and the ghastly wailing which tends to subdue the poet's prayer from harming the child.

Indeed, Kamala Das has produced a sizeable number of poems in Indo-Anglian literature. Almost all these poems share a common rendezvous. They all lie on the pedestal of love, war and sex. The treatment of the theme of love and sex is again interspersed by a sense of frustration that seems to have left a perpetual biting effect in her soul.

In my evaluation Kamala Das is found to have a high sense of modernism. She writes with rebellious attitudes denouncing old customs and traditional practices. Like every modernist who is a rebel, she also rebels against the custom ridden and orthodox society dominated by men. She would not keep her hair long but cut it short and wear trousers and which is enough a sign to defy the established order and to begin assessing of the characteristics of being a feminist. She found herself in a custom ridden and old fashioned society with patriarchal dominance. According to her, these men looked funny, repulsive and proud. They were also self-centred men who tried to look different and acted differently from womenfolk. Women, on the other hand, are dolls in the hands of men. Kamala Das could not adjust herself to this situation and, therefore, she highlighted the sensitivity of her mind through her poems. She wishes that modern women need freedom, self-respect and they are prepared to shoulder responsibility. Her poems crystallise the suppressed tensions in the minds of women, who are reluctant to speak like her. Kamala Das, therefore, has expressed her emotions freely and openly on the zone of sexual games through her poems, making herself controversial and at the same time world famous.

The Old Playhouse and Other Poems (1973): A Challenge to Patriarchy

Kamala Das published her third collection of poems entitled *The Old Playhouse and Other Poems* in 1973, and it contains 33 poems in all. Fourteen of these poems are, however, taken from the old collection, "Summer in Calcutta" and six from "The Descendants". The poems reprinted from Summer in Calcutta are : "In Love", "Love", "Summer in Calcutta", "The Freaks", "An Introduction", "My Grandmother's House", "Forest Fire", "The Wild Bougainvillea", "Corridors", "A Relationship", "The Snobs", "I Shall Someday", "Drama", and "Loud Posters", and those taken from The Descendants are : "Convicts", "Composition", "The Suicide", "The Descendants", "Palam" and "Luminol". This new volume of poems thus, has only thirteens poems to be taken into account.

This volume delves deep into the self of the poet. It tells us that love is perhaps a foot-path in experiencing and learning about one's true self. It is an avenue for the realization of one's own personality, and that the pangs and agonies associated with love are entities that cannot be done away with in life. It is mainly addressed to "you", to the husband, who wanted to hinder her from freedom of movement and action through his subtle manoeuvrings. It lodges a protest against the constraints of married life. It tries to thwart the restrictions canonised by patriarchal forces in the society. In it is felt the crystallisation of the fever of domesticity, the routine of lust, artificial comfort and male domination and can be treated as a protest to patriarchy.

Kamala Das looks for a kind of freedom; a freedom with a wider horizon; a freedom that may be treated as complete or absolute. A freedom that explores love to its zenith or to its nadir, and which is not fettered by the chains of patriarchy. However, she realizes that all these are impossible to be achieved in the human life.

"You" in the poem is possibly the husband, who wants to tame the swallow who is the woman and thus deprive her of her natural freedom. The "monstrous ego" of this husband becomes under fire herein and the poet has been reduced to a much insignificant level. As a result of his egotism, her mind becomes like "an old playhouse with all lights put out" and she feels the emptiness of the natural mirth and thinking capacity.

The following lines from *The Old Playhouse* will show as to how she spells out from freedom to imprisonment :

> . . . you call
> me wife,
> I was taught to break saccharine into your tea and
> To offer at the right moment the vitamins. Cowering
> Beneath your monstrous ego I ate the magic loaf and
> Became a dwarf. I lost my will and reason, to all your
> Questions I mumbled incoherent replies.[11]

Here the woman suggestively protests against the male ego and assertion.

The relationship of man and woman as portrayed by Kamala Das, though filled with discontentment and disharmony, is a relationship with a difference. This marriage alliance spells out exotica and the reader is made to listen with amazement. It carries us to a world of striptease and vestiges of surprises by her overpowering artistic techniques.

The frustration in married life and the emotional linkage between husband and wife are symbolically presented in it. The woman sufferer in this way realises the fallacy in married relations. She displays the tribulations of the woman who has lost anchorage in the turbulent sea of human life. The persona is denied of love and comfort. The husband all the times remains complacent, making her act according to his whims and caprices. The disgust and the anguish of the woman in her heart is clearly exhibited in a typically feminine way in one of her poems, "The Stone Age" as follows:

> Fond husband, ancient settler in the mind
> Old fat spider, weaving webs of bewilderment,
> Be kind. You turn me into a bird of stone, a granite
> Dove, you build around me a shabby drawing room,
> And stroke my pitted face absent mindedly while
> You read.[12]

The revelation that love and matrimony are poles apart

prompts Kamala Das' persona to search for a lover. Though the love affair gives her excitement in the beginning it is accompanied by disillusionment at the later stage. "The Stone Age", like "The Old Playhouse", deals with the reality of love being offered to the poetess by another man rather than by her husband. This poem portrays the husband of the woman-persona as "old fat spider" weaving "webs of bewilderment" around her and constructing the dead, dull stony wall of domesticity and thus turning her into "a bird of stone, a granite dove". The husband is the perpetual irritant, an unwelcome intruder into the privacy of the wife's mind, which is haunted by other men. When the husband goes out, she drives along the sea and climbs "the forty steps to knock at another's door". We see the act of defiance taking place vividly, the deed done, freedom asserted, heightened with the assault of the dull domesticity enveloping around her. The poetess is further charged by the energizing questions :

> . . . Ask me, every body, ask me
> what he sees in me, ask me why he is called a lion,
> A Libertine, ask me the flavour of his
> Mouth, ask me why his hands sways like a hooded snake
> Before it clasps my pubis. Ask me why like
> A great tree, filled, he stumps against my breasts,
> And sleeps. Ask me why life is short and love is
> shorter still, ask me what is bliss and what its price.
> [p. 51]

The freedom that we witness in these lines is the kind of freedom which Kamala Das has been longing for.

In most of her poems, Kamala Das tries to liberate the general lot of womenfolk by liberating herself. Her poems talk of women to be freed from the bondage of slavery in male-dominated society. She claims for perfect freedom in personal matters, chiefly in relation to love and sex. Her own personal life is a clear example of women's identity and liberty. She tries to combat against the age-old customs in the society. For this, she even deserts her own religion to maintain her status independently. According to her, men are emotionally deficient and incapable of possessing a passionate regard for concrete reality. She, therefore, celebrates a free womanhood; she gives a free individuality to her woman persona. Das" poetic career is an incessant quest for self. She is laden with sensuality and compassionate urge for sex. M.K. Naik observes her such feeling in the following remark:

> "The most obvious feature of Kamala Das" poetry is the uninhibited frankness with which she talks about sex referring nonchalantly to 'the musk of sweat between the breast", "the warm shock of menstrual blood", and even "my pubis".[13]

Hers is a different kind of protest for self-fulfilment. In the process, she releases her inner mindset with a contrast. In the poem, "*The Inheritance*", her repudiation against the fanaticism of religion is seen. This poem is bitter, ironical but not cynical. It deals with the hatred and intolerance that goes in the name of religion, whether it is Islam, Christianity, or Hinduism. What man has inherited is not love but hatred, not wisdom but babble : "This ancient/virus that we nurtured in the soul...." depicts feminism of the past, an absorbing feminist saga or how women had been regarded in the past and is regarded at present.

"Blood" is the only new poem in the longer genre just like "Composition" and "The Suicide". Here the onrush of emotions is profusely restrained. It is purely in the manner of an autobiographical sketch, and the poet's nostalgia for the old house and for the great grandmother who lived in it is convincingly evoked. However, we are to see to it that she is not trying to idealize the house nor the people associated with it; she also does not attempt to reaching out into the history of the house of a long span of three hundred years beyond what she herself knows of it. Presently, we are given the picturesque scene of an old house with the walls 'cracked and torn and moistened by the rains', the whining windows, the fallen tiles and the rats scampering hither and thither. The grandmother, who is 'really simple', religious', and proud of her 'oldest blood', is portrayed with humour and detachment.

The old house with its walls cracked and torn may also symbolize the lost happiness and the declining dignity in a woman. While the fallen tiles represent the damaged hope and aspiration of Kamala Das.

The poem is concerned with the poet's sense of death apart from the pathos of the memory of her grandmother. There is a tone of solemnity and gravity of mood indicated by its short and crisp lines. Even where Kamala Das speaks of defeat and emptiness and the irresistible darkness which is imminent, the assured clarity of outline, the serious control of nerve, and the poise of movement confirm that the poet is in command of herself in a moment of personal recollection. A pervasive and compelling sense of death and decay is clearly obvious from the following lines:

> I know the rats are running now
> Across the darkened halls
> They do not fear the dead
> I know the white ants have reached my house
> And have raised on walls
> Strange totems of burial.
> At night, in stillness,
> From every town I live in
> I hear the rattle of its death
> The noise of rafters cracking
> And the windows whine.
> I have let you down
> Old house, I seek forgiveness.[14]

Here she cherishes her placement of antiquity. She values her old house to the extent of blending up of sweet memory with that of sadness. Her leaving the house to its fate by not caring for it anymore also reveals her longing for an escape for liberty and freedom. Kamala Das, here, likens herself to

Wordsworthian Skylark which does not forget the earth – her home. Because it is as much a bird of earth as much as it is a bird of heaven. Or Shelley's Skylark that wants to escape the world as the world is full of cares; or Keatsian Nightingale of a dream world having little relationship with reality. However, a comparative study tells us that although Kamala Das may have a slight emotion or flavour associated with the above stereotypical birds, she is very much down to earth and there is an essence of truth to herself. The escapism she longs for is to isolate herself from male power. Her yearning is both humane and womanly falling within the ambit of feminist struggle.

The old house where she lived along with her grandmother and brother also refers to her Nair heritage. She often traces her blood to a royal lineage as her grandmother had once told her during her childhood:

> That we had the oldest blood,
> My brother and she and I,
> The oldest blood in the world,
> A blood thin and clear and fine
> While in the veins of the always poor
> And in the veins
> Of the new-rich men.[15]

There is a strong emotional bond between her and her great grandmother, and this is shown by the words of King Bruce:

> an inner core of identity to which she refers her name and aristocratic blood, her mother's family, life in the South and her youth in contrast to her marriage.[16]

Kamala Das is aware of the two classes – the poor and the rich – but she sounds ironical whenever such feelings come to her with intensity. The poem begins with the narration of her childhood days with her brother and grandmother who are deeply attached to the old house. As the poem proceeds, Kamala Das portrays the picture of her house as well as her relations of love. These reminiscences are a source of genuine human feelings.

She details the character of her grandmother in terms of her nature and behaviour and also the love she has for the decaying house. She is hurt on seeing the cracked and dilapidated house and the sight is as painful to her as the sight of the aged grandmother. Therefore, she promises to her,

> When I grow old, I said,
> And very very rich
> I shall rebuild the fallen walls
> And make new this ancient house[17]

But later in the poem, we come across her honest confession and realization:

> I had learnt by then
> Most lessons of defeat
> Had found out that to grow rich
> was a difficult feat.[18]

The speciality of this poem is that Kamala Das, while remembering her ancestral home and village, also feels the pulsation of the difference between her rural past and her urban present. The poet does not wish her blood to be blamed at all for not fulfilling the pledges given to her by her grandmother although her blood had inherited a stately flavour.

The blood that she possesses becomes an agency to recollect her glorious past and also carries irony of fate that the same agency cannot bring desired changes. It also hints at a feminine helplessness in the struggle against the male dominated society. The mention of the house occurs twice in the poem and describing it firstly from the grandmother's point of view and secondly from the poet's point of view. In the first description, we find that the house becomes a symbol of decay and at the same time arouses a powerful feeling of attachment and love for it. Whereas in the second phase, it causes a sense of death and becomes a symbol of inseparable past, she would never like to put a blame on her blood at any cost. There is an element of self-pity in the acceptance of her inability to retrieve and reclaim the past while upholding its glorious saga.

In the poem "Nani" we find that the poetess mingles gravity with irreverence. She is haunted by the suicide of the pregnant maid who hanged herself in the privy while the poet was yet a child. The pregnant maid, "the dark plump one, who bathed me near the well", said she and who hanged herself in the privy reflects her opinion in the following lines:

> A clumsy puppet, and when the wind blew
> Turning gently on the rope, it seemed
> To us who were children then, that Nani
> was doing, to delight us, a comic
> Dance . . . .[19]

To the children the hanging body turning gently on the rope was seemingly a dance of puppetry. They felt that Nani's body swaying as the wind blew and moved to and fro, was just entertaining them. After some years the poetess enquires of her grandmother about the dead maid. She pretends ignorance and the poetess remarks :

> With that question ended Nani. Each truth
> Ends thus with a query. It is this designed
> Deafness that turns mortality into
> Immortality, the definite into
> The soft indefinite.[20]

With the very passage of time the incident is forgotten by the grandmother, but not by the poet. We also see that the poem finally ends with a deep sense of serenity accompanied by the term "clotted peace" of the dead, but the paradox is that the imagery evolving out of the peace of the dead does not belong to the world of the dead but to that of the living world.

A question that embarrasses a person cannot be answered

by him directly as he cannot face the truth. In this regard what C.V. Venugopal remarks is worth quoting:

> The poetry of Kamala Das is full of questions that are rarely answered. They are queries about truth. But, truth, in general, is unbearable. And Kamala Das, the seeker after truth feels betrayed.[21]

Kamala Das is a poet with a high sense of curiosity. Her questioning nature in her makes her milieu well explored.

The poem "Gino" begins on a note of warning and fear. In it the kiss of a lover is compared to the bite of a krait who 'fills the bloodstream with its accursed essence." Subsequently, she becomes love-conscious, and at the same time, conscious of the sense of death which is also the essence of living. There is a conflict between the desire to experience this poisonous love, possibly love outside the wedlock, and the difficulty to 'dislodge the inherited memory of a touch'. But if this difficulty is anyhow solved, thoughts of the triumphant love haunts the poet and she dreams of 'obscure hands', of 'wardboys, sepulchral, wheeling me through long corridors/ To the x-ray room's dark interior', 'of aeroplanes/Bursting red in the sky', 'of fat/half-caste children, lovelier than Gods', and of 'Drinking wine in verandahs'. And in a sudden fit of thought, she realizes that her dreams are unreal and that the burden of the body growing unattractive and gross is more real:

> This body that I wear without joy, this body Burdened with lenience, slander, toy, owned By man of substance, shall perhaps wither, battling with My darling's impersonal lust. Or, it shall grow gross And reach large proportions before its end.[22]

The poet is obviously conjuring up here her sense of disease, death and decay of everything beautiful.

The "Glass" meanwhile focuses the attention on the proneness of the disintegration of love-experience and also of the body. There is an indepth sense of pathos when the poet says:

I went to him for half an hour
As pure woman, pure misery
Fragile glass, breaking
Crumbling. . .[23]

In contrast to the above self-hurting remark and the disadvantages of femininity, the lover avers by saying :

. . . *drew me to him*
Rudely
With a lover's haste, an armful
Of splinters, designed to hurt, and,
Pregnant with pain.[24]

In this poem, the anxiety of the poetess is voiced through a Freudian search for the misplaced father figure. She is seen moving from man to man in the search for her true home, however, there is again a sense of wasted effort purported in the prolonged search. The poem "Glass" thus becomes a clinical version as an attempt to look for him and the "misplaced" father now everywhere.

In "*The Prisoner*", the poetess has compared herself to the convict who studies his prison's geography with disbelief and hope. The situation is shown by the lines :

I study the trappings
Of your body, dear love,
For I must someday find
An escape from its snare.[25]

The term 'trappings' is very important, for it suggests "the trappings of lust from which she has to free herself to know true love" as well as "the soul's cry against its mortal dress". Usually the convict tries to escape from the prison only to return to his normal course of life. What Mrs. Das suggests here is the reality that there is no exact freedom from imprisonment of this world or of lust.

"*After the Illness*" was written after the poetess' recovery from a protracted illness. It gives us the theme of survival of herself as well as the lover's love for her. It was perhaps the deeply hidden soul that kept his love stable.

"The Millionaires at Marine Drive" is both serious and meditative in nature, its subject being the indispensable alienation of the woman. The kind of warmness which she received from the grandmother still haunts the poetess; the reason is that no man has been able to give her such an authentic love. The grandmother is shown here as an embodiment of tenderness and warmth and contrasted with her as in the following manner:

> . . . all the hands
> The great brown thieving hands groped beneath my
> Clothes, their fire was that of an arsonist's,
> Warmth was not their arm, they burnt my cities
> Down. . . .
>
> [p. 53]

The touch of her grandmother was soft and tender. Her patting and pampering had always made Kamala Das' ailing heart relieved. But the touch of her husband and other men as we have seen above, is, not at all consoling. Their touch has the similarity of the hands of "theft" which is illegal, paltry and outlawed. Groping her clothes and burning her cities down would, therefore, show the destructive incendiary devices employed by men to suppress and mar feminine interests in the society.

It is thus clear that there was, in fact, not any mental contact between her person and her husband. What she wanted above all, was a lovable "identity" with him, but her situations and circumstances brought her only the pain of growing old with a freedom she had never asked for. This poem vividly makes a shift in Kamala Das' approach to love theme; and from the grandeur of sexual love she now moves towards a general discontentment with the male character which urges to dwarf the kind of woman in her.

Kamala Das' poetry embodies agonies of women emerging from that state of subjugation and bondage, and seeking to establish their identity and the self. This collection of poems entitled, "The Old Playhouse and Other Poems", therefore, presents Indian woman in a way that has outraged the usual male sense of decency and decorum. In it she envisages a new age for woman poets, an age seeking to forge new areas, a new medium and newer modes of address constituting a total rejection of the conventional modes of poetic expression of the dominant culture. This third collection of her poems, in its entirety, hurls a scathing attack and a rebellious attitude against the male-oriented universe; and can rightfully be claimed as a challenge to patriarchy.

NOTES AND REFERENCES

1 Kamala Das, "My Story" (Delhi: Sterling Publishers Pvt. Ltd., 1976), p. 193. All the subsequent page references are to this edition.

2. Kamala Das, "The Freaks", *Summer in Calcutta*, (New Delhi: Everest Press, 1965), p. 10.

3. *Ibid.*, p. 28.

4. Kamala Das, *The Descendents* (Calcutta: Writers Workshop, 1967), p. 41.

5. *Ibid.*, p. 20.

6. *Ibid.*

7. *Op. cit.*

8. *Op. cit.*

9. *Op. cit.*

10. *Op. cit.*

11. Kamala Das, *The Old Playhouse and Other Poems* (Madras : Orient Longman, 1973), p. 1.

12. *Op. cit.*

13. M.K. Naik, *A History of Indian English Literature* (New Delhi : Sahitya Akademi, 1982), p. 208.

14. *Ibid.*
15. *Ibid.*
16. King Bruce, *Modern Indian Poetry in English* (Delhi : O.U.P., 1987), p. 149.
17. Kamala Das, "Blood" in *The Old Playhouse and Other Poems*, p. 16.
18. *Ibid.*, p. 18.
19. *Op. cit.*
20. *Ibid.*, p. 40.
21. Z.F. Molvi, "Kamala Das : Homeless in the City" in *Collected Essays on Kamala Das : A Critical Spectrum,* ed. Rajeshwar Mittapalli, Pier Paolo Piciucco (New Delhi : Atlantic Publishers and Distributors, 2001), p. 103.
22. Kamala Das, "Gino" from The *Old Playhouse and Other Poems.*
23. *Ibid.*
24. *Ibid.*
25. *Ibid.*

4

Fictional and Non-fictional Works

The feminist upsurge of Kamala Das falls also within the ambit of her novels and short stories. Though she has, to her credit, several volumes of short stories and novels in Malayalam, she writes a few of them in English. Most of those who have read all her works must agree that she is at her best in her Malayalam short stories.

Kamala Das had found by experience that her genius was not productive in the writing of novels. Her one contribution to this genre, *The Alphabet of Lust*, has made her feel that the novel was not her choice. She could not invent or construct a good plot. Nor was she a success in painting full-length portraits required in a novel. For this reason, she desists her hand a second time from the writing of the novel. In the short stories, on the other hand, no detailed plot or elaborate character delineation is required. So she takes up this as her forte and is markedly good in the depiction of characters and incidents.

Most of her portraits are of members of her Nalapat family, from her great grandmother and her famous great-uncle down to the cooks and maid-servants, and a host of other people, real and imaginary, pass before us like living persons. We see such well-drawn characters in many of her short stories.

In *Alphabet of Lust*,[1] the life story of Manasi, the frustrated wife of a government official, Amol Mitra, who looked old enough to be her father, is a long and persevering quest for identity, which, witnessing various ups and downs of life, finds its culmination in her achieving the highest and the most-coveted political office of the country – prime ministership. This quest overtakes her to an arena of assessing the limits or the freedom that a woman can carry out; which again, is one of the tenets of feminism.

The quest of the lady protagonist for success in life through the ministerial post defies her to recognize barriers, inhibitions, moral codes, and social code. Manasi becomes a poetess out of her sheer despondency in life : "her poetry had burst out of the mind of her utter hopelessness like a red lotus."[2] Her loveless, emotionally-starved, and maladjusted married life is a great disappointment to her. The fact is shown by her words: "We are not suited to each other. He is busy with his files all the time. I like people, conversation, some show of affection."[3] Sex with her husband was an act of self-mortification and, instead of showing his appreciation or gratitude for her, she, like every woman, wanted him to adore and admire her physical beauty. "She wanted him to praise the contours of her full breasts and the smooth silk of her thighs. She wanted him to smother her with surprise-gifts which had no utility value." And, this is the sensibility that runs deep in a woman and the same is wanted to be reciprocated, improved, or modified in this society of patriarchy.

The husband, on the other hand, is not conscious of the yearnings that the wife possesses, and so, he brings for her tins of ovaltine or a bottle of pickles picking them up at some reduction sale and offering them to her heraldically as though they were coveted trophies.

Kamala Das felt very unhappy and was of the view that women's sentiment could not be expressed openly and also it could not be manifested fully; besides, according to her, women saw themselves as men saw them. The real nature of women remained dormant. They were not even aware of their oppressions. They were victimised and were made to reconcile to this kind of situations because of their economic dependence on men. This shows control on women through force; the close link between women's oppression and the material conditions.

But even though the "victims" did not revolt against this kind of loopholes instituted by patriarchy, Kamala Das tries to counter oppression that despises women as women. She craves for a better environ where there will be no oppression and exploitation or the deprivation of women's rights and equality with men.

The freedom a woman ought to enjoy is further shown in her *The Alphabet of Lust*. Manasi's despair in her married life acts as a jet to her search for identity which gets a further promising stimulus and direction through her turning to Vijay, one of her old admirers, a womanizer, a young and depraved politician, now a minister, and a rising star in politics. She regretfully feels that theirs would have been an ideal pair. "We would have made an excellent pair. Poetess and Politician."[4] Vijay, who, too, is greatly charmed by her, and wants to possess and marry her, is instrumental in procuring several advantages for her. The highest literary award she receives in Delhi for her latest book of poems, according to her belief, is solely the result of Vijay's undaunted efforts. Her pleasure trip to Simla in his lustful, luscious, and luxurious company for a promised pair of diamond rings, serves to bring closer to him. In the mean time, the uninhibited sexual offers and favours purported by Manasi to those whom she meets is but one part of her quest for identity. It helps her in establishing close contacts with the prime minister, a woman-hunter, and a widower for twelve years, and wins her the greatly-cherished ministerial berth. And her sexual surrenders to those who wield great power and influence cause no remorse of conscience in her, so long as they continue to help her in climbing socially and politically. Her such nature is depicted in *The Alphabet of Lust* in the following lines:

> Vijay, I am willing to do whatever the P.M. wants me to do. It is not as if I am a chaste woman now. A *pativrata*. You saw to it that I became a mere tart. I rented out my body for a pair of diamond earrings. And hereafter for power I shall rent it out to the most influential tenant I can hope to get.
>
> [pp. 40-41]

The above lines clearly manifest on how Manasi is ever ready to sell her physique so long as she climbs the higher hierarchy of social order.

Her becoming a mistress of the prime minister, makes her obtain several rewards. She starts commanding a very great power and authority in the Government, and her less important portfolio of Information and Broadcasting is being replaced by the more important and powerful Portfolio of Home Affairs. Her political rise is never on the wane. The paralytic stroke suffered by the present prime minister, gives her the chance to hold the highest political office of the country – the prime ministership. So this is her assertion of individuality, though it causes her rift with her husband, it brings her to the highest pinnacle of success and glory.

The novel is flanked by other characters like Vijay Raje, Cyrus and Suparna. The quest for power is also readily discernible in these characters too. Vijay, for example, tries to make a niche for himself in the government, and, for this, no manipulation, no endeavour, is too intriguing and immoral for him. His obsession for becoming the greatest politician with power and influence subordinates all his other interests, including his interest in Manasi. He even sends Manasi to the prime minister's bed with a purpose as, "through her, he, Vijay Raje, was going to become the most powerful minister in the cabinet".[5] The cooperation that he extends, through fair or foul means, to the Government to stiffle and suppress all opposition is a part of his design to win appreciations as the most powerful politician. His involvement in the throwing of a bomb at Sadasivarao, his chief political rival, in one of his meetings at the C.J. Hall, the injury suffered by him through a stone hurled at him, and his death following the administration of a poisonous injection to him, is quite explicit.

Vijay Raje's shifting of attentions from Manasi to her lovely and alluring nineteen-year old daughter, Suparna, and his desire to marry her not only show his fondness of having his own preferences in personal matters but also show how women in our society are given a puppetry treatment as satisfying objects for men.

Women, in most occasions, fall as victims to gratify the carnal desires of men in these patriarchal set-ups. Manasi, going to the prime minister's bed and offering her physical body to him is not only conducive to get the highest political office but also serves as a vent for obtaining the sexual consummation of the man.

Kamala Das is so obsessed to fight the suppression of women in general. Hence, she has to come back time and again to the theme of sexual oppression. We have also observed how the foregone lines show the way male psyche treats woman as well as a willing submission on the part of woman to male arrogance. She feels restless that women go through life with an attitude of resignation and dormancy. And this practice, according to her, must be broken and a new status for women must be created at an equilibrium stage with male-folks.

Kamala Das also wrote, "A Doll for the Child Prostitute."[6] This story is the most important and interesting one. It covers 49 pages altogether and according to K. Radha, it has the stuff of a short novel rather than a long short story. In this connection, she remarks:

> "A Doll for the Child Prostitute" contains satire, irony, social criticism and even a moral. It could well have been elaborated into a novel of normal length.[7]

Since it has all the characteristics of a novel, it can be treated as a novelette.

The story is set at a Bombay brothel. It is an excellent documentary on how a brothel in any city is run. All the problems faced by the head of the house are dealt with – the competition with other houses in the neighbourhood, the sudden interference by the police, the necessity to keep the inmates well-fed, clean and free from infection, accidental pregnancy of the inmates and the difficulty of ending it, and the need to keep the police in good humour.

This novelette is much more than a documentary. It is a good story supported by a number of interesting and well drawn characters. First, and the most important of all, we have the woman who keeps the brothel, Lachmi Bai, affectionately called Ayee by the inmates. She is proud of the girls and looks after them with a sense of maternal treatment. She could legitimately claim that the girls are well-fed and clean, that they are not "filthy, five rupeewalis" like those of her rival Koushalya's in the same street. She feeds them with no dearth of vitamins. The fact is shown by the following lines from the story:

> Breakfast was served at six every morning, a heavy meal of parathas dripping with vanaspati and an egg curry. There was a glass of milk to top the meal. After partaking of this meal the girls normally curled up on their mats and fell asleep until it was time again for the next meal which was at two. It was only after five that they stirred themselves to attend to their toilets. The bath was elaborate and afterwards their hair was decked with strings of flowers, and, rouge was rubbed into the skin of their cheeks to make them look healthy
>
> [p. 85]

We see from the above that Ayee Lachmi Bai takes every precaution to make her girls look healthy and attractive. She also knows that her business of the world of prostitution can only be progressed this way. She, therefore, takes the girls to a doctor every week to ensure that they are not sources of infection. She loves them in her own way and they in turn look upon her as a kind guardian who possesses motherly care.

Of the inmates, the best looking and the most educated is Mira who keeps a close attachment with a young college student. He visits her daily and spends hours with her, teaching her politics, and the Gita Govinda, etc. Because of the love offered to her by the college student, Mira wants to reciprocate her love for him. She no longer wants to entertain her visitors any more; she wants to free herself from the chains of the world of prostitution and so, she ultimately asserts her feminine protest against male chauvinism by eloping with the college student.

Although they elope, their love and romance are knocked out of them in the police station. She is brought back to the brothel, but this time, she loses her room which was the best in the house to the dark Saraswati after her escapade.

We have learnt from the story how much the two lovers were obsessed. There was always an air of sadness in their countenance whenever their discourse was over. They cried helplessly after every rendezvous. Their poor condition is reflected in the words which the weeping Mira tells her Ayee:

> He said that he had to sell his pen to visit me. He has no income of his own. He comes here saving his lunch-allowance and his bus fare. He loves me. . . .
>
> [p. 79]

Women in our society are forcibly pushed to undergo flesh-trade even if they don't want to. They are enduced to perform the tasks which they don't really want but they are forced to do the works for survival and for filling up their own bellies.

Mira is coerced by cruel fate from her very childhood to grow up in the atmosphere and the tradition of the world of prostitution. She has to compromise and adapt to the kind of environs she has been thrust upon despite the discontentment she may have in her heart. She feels that she is in the wrong placement. To assert her quest for freedom of existence, she vehemently tries to undo herself from the fetters of the brothel-house resulting in her elopement with the college boy.

In the story we also find the two child-prostitutes Sita and Rukmani, who have not even attained puberty, are consciously or unconsciously, made to profess the abominable trade of prostitution. Their world presents a series of snapshots depicting the horried life of the unfortunate inmates of a house of disrepute, a sickening, dehumanizing world of dirt and disease, sloth and scandal, and the pain and the penury inflicted to these inmates.

The helpless orphans, Sita and Rukmani, are too young to realise the full implication of the profession they are practising. Sita was thrown into the profession after all her family members died because of cholera four years ago. And Rukmani was kept there by her own mother, Anasuya out of wretchedness and starving condition at home, and also, most inevitably, because of the unbecoming behaviour of her step-father. The remark she gives on the day Rukmani was kept in the brothel of Lachmi Bai (Ayee) runs as follows:

> I would not have taken any money from you, Ayee, but we are practically starving at home. The baby is given nothing but tea and may be a banana at noon.
>
> [p. 68]

Out of sheer innocency the two children land up in this kind of dehumanizing and sickening trade of disrepute. Feminists thus desire to fight for such kind of oppression and exploitation against the 'fair-sex' in a system of patriarchal dominance. They want women to stand up and fight against this injustice. They call on women to resist marginalisation and passivisation.

The two characters portrayed by Kamala Das as Sita and Rukmani in "A Doll for the Child Prostitute" shows us how innocent children and women are oppressed in a system of male hegemony. These two helpless orphans, particularly Rukmani, is too young to decipher the significance of the job she is doing. Let us unfold the discourse they exchange to each other when she joins the brothel for the first time.

> "I cannot sleep in the day", said Rukmani. Sita laughed loudly and held on to her stomach as though it was about to burst. "You are so innocent. Do you think we can sleep at night in this house? We shall all be so busy entertaining the visitors." "Visitors at night ?" asked Rukmani "who will come at night ?" Sita could not control her laughter. "Oho ho", she laughed . . . .
>
> Rukmani kept her satchel of books on the mat meant for her and Sita. "Men come to do things here", said Sita. "What things ?" asked Rukmani. She was thinking

of her step-father and the pain she had experienced. [p. 70]

The above lines inflame the readers with pathos and a sense of discontentment. The scenic situation brings forth a curiosity and an impulse to immediately rectify the wrongs taking place in our society. It provokes our thought to stand up and voice against the sexual harassment of the young females done especially with masochistic tendencies. It drives us forward with a zeal to correct such mistakes and punish the wrong persons.

The characters delineated in these short stories appear real and seem to be living persons of flesh and blood. These characters, therefore, win the pity and the sympathy of the readers and activate in them a strong bond of audacity with an inclination to abolish the flaws and errors of the phallic power.

The works of Kamala Das also supply the raw material to be pragmatic and also to ruminate what is antithetical to Roland Barthes' statement, "The text dies with the author". It is to see to it that there is progression evolving out of the reading of her text. The text should, with the spirit of the author, improve the suffering lot of the women-folk. It must be an avenue to interpret the text focusing on their grievances, subjugations, suppressions and exploitations, etc. Hence, it demands, on the part of the scriptor, to tactfully explain such oppressions and find a way to curb the already deplorable conditions of these women sect.

This text is a rendezvous to highlighting all the oppressions done to women in general and to explore their concealed emotions as seen on the portraits of Mrs. Das. Rukmani, for instance, represents the most pathetic figure in the brothel as she is too young to know anything about the happening in the house. Then there is the sweet and fragile Sita who becomes pregnant and meets her own death due to a crude operation of abortion. And yet, the Police Inspector manages to certify that the poor girl's death was a burst appendix.

The manner in which Kamala Das tells her stories comes

like a "combing operation". Her narratives are powerful enough to provide suspense and scintillation. In the meantime, when we 'deconstruct' the specific characters in the persons of Sita and Rukmani, it shifts to any child, daughter, niece or young girl who could have similarly been forced into the trade of child prostitution against her wish. Such practices should be removed from our society. The pangs and the agonies endured by these girls must be given a timely intervention. The authorities concerned must not stay aloof or shy away from such occurrences.

Short fictions by Indian women continue to explore the different ways in which women try to survive and the way they cope themselves with the society, their responses and expectations evolving out of marriage call for careful consideration. In the attempt to establish their identity, they have launched various protests and rebellions within the boundary of marriage. Marriage, again, is an indispensable obligation to the middle-class Indian women. So they cannot abstain from it. The days they spend in agony, the suffering they receive, the hardships, which, in few cases are incongruous, are found culminated within the institution of marriage. Myriads of feminine protests in a pluralistic society like India, are found in plenty and varied over the years in the hands of writers of different temperaments and viewpoints.

Kamala Das' "A Little Kitten"[8] is a short story. It explains how sexual attraction diminishes in a couple after marriage. The deliberate omission of names for the husband and wife makes this story a generalized relationship for all marriages. In the beginning of the story, married life is presented like a perpetual honeymoon with its picturesque scene of a middle-class character. However, with the passage of time, the charms of marriage begins to fade, and the wife starts longing for a pet. See how the author avers of the husband and the wife in the following remark:

> ... at Dadar, she told her husband that she felt miserable and lonely from eight in the morning to six in the evening while he worked in the insurance firm at the heart of the city. If you could get me a pet, she murmured,

> nestling closer to his chest, a little kitten, even a little kitten would be such a comfort....[9]

The deterioration of the value of marriage is palpable. Here the wife becomes so lonely that even a pet like a kitten would have been such a good companion in the absence of her husband. But he does not give much attention to her wish. He simply thinks, "what a sweet and innocent creature he had married" (38). The term "creature" and not "woman" should be marked and taken into consideration. The reason is that many a woman are treated below the level of human beings. They are likened to be objects for satisfying the sexual urge of men. The husband simply amuses himself by playing with her instead of endorsing her the slightest idea on finding a kitten for her. He plays with her "until she rolled over on their double bed and screamed out for mercy. You are killing me, please stop, PLEASE STOP." (38). The truth of her cry does not reach him; however, her boredom, her loneliness, and her discontentment at being treated like a toy, are killing her.

The wife is just a plaything for the husband, so he tires of her, and the quarrels, and the lack of communication separate them apart. The wife becomes increasingly frustrated and disoriented. She no longer takes bath in the evenings. The freshness has gone out of her, and no longer hangs strands of jasmine on her plait. These flowers are an image of the lost happiness and of unfulfilled hopes. The later details also add to the sense of the disintegration of the marriage. For instance, the "new crease on her brow which sliced the red bindi into two halves"(39), his coming home "dead drunk" one evening, her tearing of her sari "into shreds" – again the smoke from the chimney of the neighbouring mill that darkens her skin are evidences of a life sans happiness and sans peace.

Besides, the husband no longer takes any interest in sex games with his wife. So he gives his secretary expensive gifts and also takes her out to private places like the restaurants "where they could sit half-concealed behind potted cacti" (40). The wife with a tinge of the disillusioned relationship of the marriage, wishes to go back to her parents, but he dissuades her from going there as he is scary of what her parents would say. This deteriorated bond between the husband and the wife is seen by other characters in the story as is shown in the following lines:

> Even the old Maharastrian woman who used to wash the vessels for her in the morning, began to wonder what had gone wrong. She had lost her bridal freshness.[10]

Later in the story, we find that the wife comes back to life. She dresses up again, smiles at him, look pink and healthy with a red scratch above her breasts; and this scratch is taken to be the handiwork evolving out of her finding a kitten for herself to play with, a new interests in life. She does not answer when the husband asks if she has found a kitten, but she simply smiles and looks up at the "dusky sky" (40) with all its association of freedom and mystery, though to him they are only "some clouds, some smoke". (40) The husband's "infidelity" on sexual matters, too is a pleasure and a game to him.

This infidelity is experienced amongst many of our couples today. So the loneliness which the wife experiences is also the loneliness which every woman faces in this society of male dominance.

The deterioration of the relationship of the couples after marriage, the disenchantment wrought by this institution of nuptiality in terms of mutual indifference, distrust, unwariness, negligence, etc., are on the rise. The worsening relations of husbands and wives, the isolation and the alienation associating especially with "fair sex" must be given a proper consideration and assimilative analysis.

Women are often marginalised. They are invariably found in many of the circumstances and situations which are exploitative as well as suppressive. They, therefore, need a helping hand to shift the position they are occupying, and must be given better avenues to combat subjugation or suppression whereby they, too, could enjoy the privileges of equality and liberty. The de facto erroneous position of these so-called 'others' needs a change so as to bring them at par with male chauvinism.

Kamala Das' *My Story*[11] has won her a colossal cognizance as a poet and a writer. It will not be an exaggeration to say that she is the most controversial Indian poet writing in English because of the publication of this autobiography. The very qualities of forthrightness and expressiveness found in the story demand laudability and appreciation. But few of our genuine readers saw the work as a woman's tale of woe, or paid attention to its theme of loneliness or discontentment. Here, we can see how by the very act of defining female space, she was recognized as a threat to the then existing adherents of patriarchal practices. As a result, many critics including her own relatives had to file suit for her unprecedented writing. Severe critical dissent and adverse publicity were hurled against her as a consequence of which she had to withdraw herself. Thus, the writer who had attempted to define female space becomes different and unsure of her intrinsic worth. She feels mandatory to provide an explanation for her work. In her preface to *My Story*, she explains the reasons for her writing thus:

> The doctor thought that writing would distract my mind from the fear of a sudden death, and, besides, there were all the hospital bills to be taken care of.

Despite the public outcry, social disparagement and the insecurity she might have felt, this text serves as the "central-text" for all the critics in matters of such genres as psychology, sociology and psychoanalysis with regard to women. It can also be taken as the basis for the ramification of approaches including Marxist and other diverse post-structuralist theorists besides defining masculinity and feminity.

With the launching of this book, many changes are seen from the perspective of feminist ideologies in Indian writings in English. The emphasis on "female-ego" gets broadened, women in the society become popular and more women writing begins to appear in public. Today, women in India can freely mention the term "sex" without any inhibition. It is no longer a taboo or a word to impinge feminine dignity, nor can it degrade womanly image. Contrastingly, by mentioning this term, a woman can openly pursue her rights as an individual and as an equal being to live with dignity. She can freely stand up and fight against the unjust codes of phallocentric systems. This free exercise of expressions and open confessions might have not been possible had there been no personality as Kamala Das. She has outrightly carved out a new route for all feminist writers to drive home feminist sensibilities. She did this at the cost of discarding traditional canons and the ethos of an Indian womanhood. However, she does not in the least regret for what she has done as she emphatically describes in the preface of her autobiography given below :

> This book has cost me many things that I held dear, but I do not for the moment regret having written it. I have written several books in my lifetime, but none of them provided the pleasure the writing of My Story has given me. [Preface]

Kamala Das could decipher that delving deep into her own self would create a uniqueness in the literary scene. For this reason, she takes the risk in materialising her own story in the book form. Only by writing an expression she knew that the woman writer would succeed in breaking down existing social power structures and create a place for herself in the world of masculine hierarchies. The woman writer, as she understands, could thereby alter her existing marginalized position and accept her rightful role as a significant part of the society. By writing the self, the woman writer could challenge the accepted notions of feminity and redraft general opinion on the feminine mystique and so she took up the art of writing, about herself.

The very title - *My Story* — impresses us and there is an indication of amorous scintillation that comes with a big bang. It is shown by the scene of the wedding night.

> The rape was unsuccessful but he comforted me when I expressed my fear that I was perhaps not equipped for sexual congress. . . . Again and again throughout

> that unhappy night he hurt me and all the while the Kathakali drums throbbed duly against our window and the singers sang of Damayanti's plight in the jungle.
>
> [p. 93]

The tone of her expression arouses sexuality and sex-intrigues. Excitement is one of the irresistible characteristic traits in her narratives. As we have seen in the above lines, she demonstrates her own story with a tinge of seduction. Her exposition of narration can be likened to Ulyssean voyage. Just as Ulysses meets many women such as Circe and other enchantresses on his return journey from the Trojan War, Kamala Das also encounters a number of men other than her husband and develops extra marital affairs with them in the later stage of her married life.

Kamala Das got married to a person who was interested only in her body, and used it for his gratification of carnal desire; but his lust seemed to be insatiable. During the engagement period, while he was posted in Bombay she narrates her experience as: "whenever he found me alone in the room, he began to plead with me to bare my breasts and if I did not, he turned brutal and crude. His hands bruised my body and left blue and red marks on the skin"(87). He was indeed, well-versed in the art of sex games that he narrated to her the sexual exploits he had shared with some of the maidservants in his house in Malabar. Kamala Das had also hoped that marriage would give her altogether, a different picture : "I had expected him to take me in his arm and stroke my face, my hair, my hands and whisper loving words. I had expected him to be all that I wanted my father to be, and my mother. I wanted conversation, companion and warmth. Sex was far from my thoughts. I had hoped that he would remove with one sweep of his benign arms, the loneliness of my life"(87). The nuptial tie mentioned by her father as finding a "mate" also saddened and depressed her. The word "mate" with its earthly connotations made her uneasy and yet, she could not express her discontentment openly and her such predicament is voiced in the following words:

> "I would not tell my father that I had hoped for a more tranquil relationship with a hand on my hair and a voice in my ear, telling me that everything was going to be all right for me. I had no need at all for the rough hands riding up my skirts or tearing up my brassiere"
>
> [p. 87]

The above lines reflect the utter helplessness of Mrs. Das. She had hoped that marriage could be a tranquil relationship; a unison of two hearts in love and tenderness, a mutual understanding between the wife and the husband, etc. But contrary to her aspirations, it turned out to be a reality of illusioned taste in which she received little or no attention from her husband. As early as 1949, Simone de Beauvoir wrote in *The Second Sex*:

> Women do not set themselves up as subject and hence have erected to virile myth in which their projects are reflected; they have no religion or poetry of their own: they still dream through the dreams of men.[12]

What Simone de Beauvoir remarked in 1949 seems still relevant to our womenfolk today. Seemingly, what a man cannot do must also not be done by a woman. These women seem to have been barred from expressing what they like or feel. Feminists, therefore, are trying hard to draw up a road-map for themselves. They try to define themselves and create a world of their own; a world in which their mouths are not gagged to express their hidden emotions but can freely raise their voice to the maximum decibel height.

Their strategy to the realisation of this dream is given to writing. Through writing, they believe, could a woman writer succeed in breaking down the existing social power structures and create a place for herself in the world of masculine hegemony. By writing herself, Kamala Das also believes that she could challenge the accepted notions of the female despondency and find a new footpath to translate or interpret her dreams. Rosalind Brackenbury, a staunch feminist, holds the following view:

> Nobody writes in a vacuum, away from the political

> and social structures in which we live. We breathe the air of today's thought, we digest it in everything we read and consider; also, we create it. This is largely the role of women today : to create, present and consider a new world.[13]

Kamala Das also tries her level best to create a new horizon wherein she can freely give vent to her hidden emotions, and freely express them. The result is the publication of this most controversial autobiography *"My Story"*.

When Kamala Das felt betrayed, lonely and disappointed at her husband's place; and when she found that her love was "like alms looking for a begging bowl which only sought for a receptacle"(124), an Italian, Carlo, came into her life. She fell in love with him who is an extremely handsome young man, at Khar gymkhana, where she had gone in the evening to play tennis. "The evening sun lit up his grey eyes. The gloss of his skin and the beauty of his smile made me feel all of a sudden so awestruck, so humble. . . ." [p. 119]

> Love transformed her life and she described that her . . . "days were filled with incredible sweetness. On the porch the Rangoon creepers bloomed, the tender pinks looking white in the evening's shadows. I hung a brass lamp in the porch and lit it every evening". [p.120]

> "One evening when I was seated on the top step of the porch, the grey-eyed friend came to sit at my feet. His lips had a tremor which delighted me. I hope you are not falling in love with me, I said, smiling down at him. He hid his face in the folds of my sari. Outside my sons were playing with the neighbour's children. Inside our drawing room my husband was working on his files." [p.120]

Her mention of the lips of the lover boy with tremor is enough a significance that she has some sex appeal of him. This amorous perception is also associated by a mark of daringness and bravery because the rendezvous she mentions in the story takes place adjacent to her husband which is evidenced by the line - "Inside our drawing room my husband was working on his file."

She goes on to demonstrate yet another moving experience to add to her courage and valour:

> During that summer while the Gulmohurs burnt the edges of the sky, he dressed my hair with white flowers plucking them from beneath my window. What did he want from me? Once or twice standing near him with his arms around my shoulders I whispered I am yours, do with me as you will, make love to me. . . . but he said, no, in my eyes you are a goddess, I shall not dishonour your body. [p. 121]

From the above we come to observe that Kamala Das' revelation on man-woman relationship is to the maximum level because the consummation of love completes the whole affairs of a man and a woman who are in love. Her offer of her body to her lover "to make love" is an expression which is not decorous to a modest Nair woman. But she freely expresses this fact or whatever she has in her mind. Her expression finds its culmination in terms of her anecdotes, *tale, story, narrative, yarn, sketches*, etc.

In a way, she deconstructs the patriarchal power structures by assassinating or violating the canons framed by the pro-misogynic society. Kamala Das wants to delineate all the events and situations that she comes across; and she shows them to the readers without any reticence. She, as a feminist, confronts the inconvenient restrictions which envelop the "fair sex" and draws a new term of reference, an entirely different structural framework for woman writing. Like all feminists call for a new language, Kamala Das also joins the slogan that would assist in expressing female experiences. Elaine Showalter explains the programme thus :

> The programme of gynocritics is to construct a female framework for the analysis of women's literature, to develop new models based on the study of female experience, rather than adapt male models and stories.[14]

The works of Kamala Das – both poetry and Prose – are startlingly unconventional in the Indian context. Yet, she persistently pursued her writing without ever being bothered whether her husband or community liked it or approved of it. Truly, it was her writing which provided her with an outlet for her hidden discontentment, hurts, humiliations and grief.

Love was what she had longed for, and Carlo was not the only one. She was overflowing with love and she made an offering of it to others as well. She must have experienced all phases of love : platonic, sensuous, serene, cynical, conjugal, illicit, picturesque and lusty like that of John Donne because she had even tried 'adultery' for sometime.

She also got infatuated with a literary-minded friend with whom she enjoyed conversing on literary subjects. She gave him gilded volumes of Lawrence Hope. Her relationship with Carlo also continued. She visited him at his hotel. Her longing for love was incessant like an ever flowing spring. She would not give up her search for a true and ideal lover. She says,

> I loved as men love their women, but I yearned for change, a new life. I was looking for an ideal lover. I was looking for the one who went to Mathura and forgot to return to his Radha. Perhaps I was seeking the cruelty that lies in the depths of a man's heart. Otherwise why did not I get my peace in the arms of my husband ? (180)

Kamala Das' search for her ideal lover was a failure because it cannot be found in the human form. No matter how hard she tried, she could not achieve what she had been looking for. She began to realise this reality with the onset of middle age, bringing with it a gross skin and a haggard face. She began to doubt whether she could "lure a charming male into a complicated satisfying love affair with the right words, the right glances, the right gestures ?" Whether her time as a charmer was finished and gone ? "Then with the force of a typhoon", she says, "he conquered me, the last of my lovers, the most notorious of all, the king of all kings, the bison among animals, the handsome dark one with a tattoo between his eyes".

[pp.187-188]

She further described this man who had seduced and titillated her in the following words:

> He was coming out of a cloth shop at Churchgate and I was walking in. His face was familiar to me. I stared at him in fascination. There were several stories circulating about his innumerable love affairs and his sexual prowess. In my eyes he was a magnificent animal.
>
> [p. 188]

Kamala Das who had for long craved for a tender love-relationship finally got fascinated by this man, who was known for his fabulous lusts. Having met him at the airport for a second time, she says,

> He drew me to him as a serpent draws its dazed victim. I was his slave. That night I tossed about in my bed thinking of his dark limbs and of his eyes glazed with desire. Very soon we met and I fell into his arms.
>
> [p. 190]

Whatever Kamala Das writes, is tilted on the realm of carnal hungers. Her depiction of the relationship of man and woman is unique although the canvass that she employs is very much within the discipline of Indian ethos and flavour. She explores her body as well as the biological sensations in sexual terms. By delving deep into her own self she becomes the mouthpiece for every Indian woman in terms of the tales of discontentment, victimization, agony, exploitation, disgrace, abuse and of course, sex experiences.

Her search for ideal love coerced her to develop extramarital affairs and a heterogeneous mixture of lovers outside the wedlock. She did this at the cost of defying her family background, culture, tradition, the modesty and the chastity of a Nair woman which again is an important feminist principle.

Love, according to Kamala Das, is not a mere physical exercise; but should be accompanied by the fulfilment of the spirit. For this reason she fell in love with many lovers hoping to achieve an ideal love. But her search came to be a failure because real love or true love cannot be achieved in the physical form. Realizing fully on the impossibility of finding real love in the human form, she reconciles it with Radha-Krishna myth or the Mira-Krishna relationship; and finally yearns for Lord Krishna as her icon.

From the foregone analysis, we come to know that Kamala Das is very much a confessional poet. Her open confession has made her personality manifest in its stark nakedness. *My Story*, therefore, gives a perspective of her whole individuality including her sex life, feminine longings and forthrightness.

The oodles of love-experience she portrays associated with its peculiarity and incongruity might, according to some critics, be understood with reference to the sociological dimension offered by her Nair lineage. Sunanda P. Chavan in this regard, puts it in the following lines:

> The Nair society has the matrilineal, matrilocal organisation and did not hinder the plurality of husbands to a Nair woman. Of course, it treated marital relations with increasingly rigidity from the end of the 19th century.[15]

Whatever the case may be, Kamala Das has carved out a new route with an unprecedented zeal through her writing especially for the women-writers of India so as to give vent to their depreciated values and to redress their feminine grievances. This autobiography with which she puts myriads of her thoughts and actions has given an impetus as an example for every woman to protest and rebel against the unjust forces of patriarchy. It also offers one to write freely and openly.

In the course of my research investigation, I have found her to be sensitive, bold and transparent in articulating her temperament or personal anguish. Her vital effort to expose man-woman relationship in its full complexity has given a new horizon enough to inflame the outlook of the feminist writers.

The report I have furnished here will also serve as a very useful source of information in furthering investigation and enquiry into Kamala Das' oeuvre for the young scholars; and it would not be an exaggerated statement that she has modernised the Indian psyche on women writing.

NOTES AND REFERENCES

1. Kamala Das, *Alphabet of Lust*, (New Delhi : Orient Paperbacks, 1976).
2. *Ibid.*, p. 10.
3. *Ibid.*
4. *Ibid.*, p. 15.
5. *Ibid.*, p. 60.
6. Kamala Das, "A Doll for the Child Prostitute" in *Padmavati, the Harlot and Other Stories* (New Delhi : Sterling Paperbacks, 1992).
7. K. Radha, *The Short Stories of Kamala Das: An analysis in Indian Women Novelists* (New Delhi: Prestige Books, Set II, Vol. I, 1993) p. 197.

   * All the subsequent page references are to this edition.
8. Kamala Das, "A Little Kitten", in *Padmabati, the Harlot and Other Stories* (New Delhi : Sterling Paperbacks, 1992).
9. *Op. cit.*, p. 38.
10. *Ibid.*, p. 39.
11. Kamala Das, My Story (New Delhi : Sterling Publishers Pvt. Ltd., 1976)

    * All the subsequent page references are to this edition.
12. Simone de Beauvoir, *The Second Sex*, 1949 rept. (London : Picador, 1988), p. 174.
13. Rosalind Brackenbury, *Women and Fiction : How We Present Ourselves and Others, In Other Worlds*, (London: Hutchinson, 1989), p. 56.
14. Usha V.T., "One Woman's Autography : Kamala Das's *My Story*"

in collected essays in Kamala Das, A Critical Spectrum ed. Rajeshwar Mittapalli and Pier Paolo Piciucco (New Delhi : Atlantic Publishers and Distributors, 2001), p. 4.

15. Sunanda P. Chavan, "The Moderns 11 : Kamala Das" in *A Study of Indian Women Poets in English, The Fair Voice* (New Delhi: Sterling Publishers Pvt. Ltd. 1984), p. 67.

5

Renaissance in Language and Style

Many factors accumulate to contribute to Kamala Das' language, diction, technique and style. She makes a judicious choice of words and makes her language captivating so as to impress her readers. She can freely express things to her heart's contentment and can also delineate whatever she wishes through her chosen words.

Although she receives no formal education or no pompous university degree yet, she is a conscientious artist who is mainly guided by her impulse and instinct for using precise and harmonious words. She is also aware of the value of words and so she makes subtle distinctions in picking up or turning down her words and phrases. The choice of words, phrases and expressions render her poetry beautiful and precise.

In order to have a detailed study of the language, diction, technique and style of Mrs. Das, it would be viable to have a briefing of what these things mean. Language may be defined as:

> The human use of spoken or written words as a communication system, while the choice of words to fit their context may mean diction. Technique, on the other hand, refers to the procedure, skill or art used in a particular task, while a distinctive and identifiable form in an artistic medium such as music, architecture or literature, etc., is called style.[1]

Interestingly, the society that Kamala Das belongs to

is a matrilineal society, not a patrilineal one. But matrilineality, as pointed out by Kate Millet, "does not constitute an exception to patriarchal rule, it simply channels the power held by males through female descent — e.g. the "Avanculate."[2] So, the culture to which Kamala Das belongs is also much inclined to the myth of male superiority as any patriarchal culture. But the problem is that Kamala Das cannot flatly reconcile with male-power to accept him as the "referent" while accepting the female as the "other", "alien" or "sex-object".

It is, therefore, Kamala Das' share of the cup to launch a scathing attack to patriarchy through her creative writings. She draws the stuff from her own situations as a wife at Calcutta or at Bombay or at her Nalapat House. But her writing had to be carried out under a pseudonym to hide her identity. She did this so as to adjust herself with the then existing society. In this regard the following lines from *My Story* tells how she had to be a masquerader:

> Whenever a story appeared in a journal I ran with it to my bedroom to lie down and read it, for my heart used to thump so with excitement to see my name in print. I used to publish poems in the Illustrated Weekly but under the name K. Das because I suspected the editor to be prejudiced against women writers.[3]

The above lines verify how women folk are subjected to hide their identities or mask their personalities like the changing colours of a chameleon to avoid prejudice of men.

The language used by Kamala Das evolves out of her relationship with her family, relatives, husband and the society at large. Her language is sometimes pornographic and domestic. The resources of her language and diction are taken from her own situation as a wife and as a poetess and they are, therefore, shades of her own locality and regionalism. When she wants to point out the helplessness and passivity of women in the male-dominated society, she assigns the subject positions to the males. Women are assigned the object positions or she makes use of the passive forms of the verbs which shows the passivity of women. She uses *vers libre* or free verse to suit her situations and ample freedom. At the level of lexical items, the nouns like "slave", "toy", "bride", "virgin", "prostitute", "wife", "doll", "puppet", "mother", "women", "convict", "prisoner", "sex", "lust", "desire", "love", "day-dreams", "death", "blood", etc. are the repeated ones and there is also a close link of these words with the situations of women in this society of masculinised culture.

Kamala Das uses irony as one of her powerful stylistic devices. She uses it very effectively and regularly to drive home the oppressions inflicted to women by the power of the phallus. For her, irony serves as an impetus to attack the masculine violence and the sexist culture's efforts to exploit, passivise and marginalize women. Mention also must be made, in this regard, of the use of the dots that she often makes use of. The dots used by her reveal the eloquence of silence. Truly speaking the unexpressed things in Kamala Das is sometimes more effective than the expressed things. Averring of her language, in "An Introduction", she says :

> The language I speak
> becomes mine, its distortions, its queerness
> All mine, mine alone. It is half English, half
> Indian, funny perhaps, but it is honest,
> It is as human as I am human, don't
> You see ?
>
> [*Summer in Calcutta*, p. 59]

Kamala Das' use of the English language is so bold and daring. She uses it against the wish of her friends and visiting cousins. She defies all suggestions and makes use of it with grimness and daringness. Commenting on the use of this language, Iqbal Kaur states:

> . . . it is as defiant, as authentic as she herself is. There can be no two opinions that her verse is as free as Kamala Das herself. In poetry, she defies all restrictions of metre and rhythm, just as she defies the oppressive social reality and her prose is no less energetic, no less frank than the writer herself.[4]

As Iqbal Kaur has rightly pointed out, Kamala Das defies the rules on metre and rhythm; she also avoids the use of punctuations and syntactical applications in her writings. Her superficial treatment of syntax may be observed from the following lines:

> I compromised myself with every sentence I wrote and thus I burnt all the boats that would have reached me to security. What did I finally gain from life ? Only the vague hope that there are a few readers who have loved reading my books although they have not wished to inform me of it. It is for each of them that I continue to write, although the abusive letters keep pouring in.
>
> [*My Story*, pp. 220-21]

Pinpointing some of the deficiencies of the above lines, Shyamala A. Narayan argues and comments as follows:

> The phraseology is clumsy, and one is surprised that a practising poet can write such adolescent stuff. At places, the choice of words is wrong - "reached me to security"- reached is not the correct verb in the context, "taken" or 'helped me reach' would have been better".[5]
>
> [*My Story*, pp. 220-221]

Kamala Das who could not go for higher studies or for higher scholastic achievements, suffers from the paucity of the rules of grammar. She herself understands the dearth of scholasticism in her and testifies her inefficiency in *My Story* as follows:

> I typed nearly a thousand words a week. I wrote about the subjects the editors asked me to write on, fully aware that I was uneducated by the usual standards and that I had no business meddling in grave matters.
>
> [p. 218]

Despite the inefficiency Mrs. Das suffers here and there, she is undeniably a love-poet. Love is what she has been looking for; and would not give up unless she finds an authentic love. But being a poet of love essentially, she sometimes feels that words are a nuisance in love-making.

> All around me are words, and words and words,
> They grow on me like leaves, they never
> Seem to stop their slow growing
> From within . . . but I tell myself, words
> Are a nuisance, beware of them, they
> Can be so many things . . . .
>
> [*Summer in Calcutta*, p. 11]

Although we do not know the precise moods and sentiments conveyed by these words growing like leaves, they can be interpreted as the irresistible rise of feminism. These words which are a nuisance and which "never seem to stop their slow growing from within" would also mean the gradual spreading of feminist theories and ideologies everywhere even though they may be a nuisance to male chauvinists, who hold strongly to unreasoned opinions about the way men and women should behave, and the parts they should play in life, especially believing that men are better than women.

Kamala Das speculates that these words spring from 'a silence, somewhere deep within' to manifest themselves without inhibition. In another poem, "Convict," she demonstrates the futility of words during and after intense love-making:

> There were no more
> Words left, all words lay imprisoned
> In the ageing arms of night.
>
> [*The Descendants*, p. 32]

Here the language of love becomes silent after their love has been consummated to the fullest extent. In real life, human beings enjoy the pleasure of love fully and to the maximum, but the pleasures of love when enjoyed in excess give rise to a feeling of intense satiety and disillusionment. We see Kamala Das and her lover lying fatigued and speechless after intense love-making and this eyeshot contradicts the art-form of Keatsian line, "For ever panting and for ever young" taken from his "Ode on a Grecian Urn", where the two lovers' passion will always remain and their love will never fade unlike real life.

From a feminine perspective, the writing of Kamala Das seems unprecedented and un attempted before by other Indo-English writers. The uninhibited frankness in her expression with regard to the question of the use of 'language' may be rehighlighted from her well known poem, "An Introduction" wherein she writes about herself as follows:

> I am Indian, very brown, born in
> Malabar, I speak three languages, write in
> Two, dream in one. Don't write in
> English, they said, English is not your mother-tongue. Why not leave
> Me alone, critics, friends, visiting cousins,
> Everyone of you? Why not let me speak in
> Any language I like?

and in the later part of the same poem, she says:

> It voices my joys, my longings, my
> Hopes, and it is useful to me as cawing
> Is to crows or roaring to the lions, it
> Is human speech, the speech of the mind that is
> Here and not there, a mind that sees and hears and
> Is aware. Not the deaf, blind speech
> Of trees in storms or of monsoon clouds or of rain or the
> Incoherent mutterings of the blazing
> Funeral pyre.

Summer in Calcutta, p. 59.

The above lines convince us that Kamala Das is all set to use the English language as a medium of her creative writings. She, therefore, makes a powerful appeal for her use of the language. Whether she "dreams" in it or in Malayalam is a different question, but she writes in English with an easy command and awful skill. "An Introduction" shows us that it has more bearing on her use of the "English" and the protest she receives from others than with that of any other languages.

The diction of Kamala Das is, broadly speaking, both lyrical and natural. Simplicity and lucidity are its hallmarks. It is hardly ever wrapped up in philosophical broodings or mystical abstractions. Her use of lyricism is also enhanced by the following passage:

> ; is I who laugh, it is I who make love
> And then, feel shame, it is I who lie dying
> with a rattle in my throat, I am sinner,
> I am saint, I am the beloved and the
> Betrayed.
> [An Introduction, Summer in Calcutta, p. 60]

The last part of the lines becomes something like an invocation and speaks in the voice of an enraptured sage of the Upanishads. Here language has been put to a superb use, and it does not fail the emotions of the poetess. The poem, "The Suicide" is also marvellous and an exemplary piece of lyricism and simplicity:

> O sea, I am fed up
> I want to be simple
> I want to be loved
> And
> If love is not to be had,
> I want to be dead.....
> [*The Descendants*, p. 8]

Kamala Das uses a language which is that of a poet and does not "search for pretty words which dilute the truth". She, being primarily a poet, makes use of expressive symbols and images in her prose works also; some of which like hospital, house, window and toys recur in her writing. Her recurrent use of the Krishna — Mira myth is noteworthy as it helps her to impart significance to the portrayed relationship.

"A Doll for the Child Prostitute" could be the fitting example, because its very title, "Doll" is the bribe used to win over a child. Furthermore, the descriptive terms, "Doll" and "Child", suggest innocency which is opposite to what is revealed by the story. We may also agree to the fact that Rukmani, the child symbolises innocence and the Inspector stands for experience.

The writings of Kamala Das present Indian woman in a way that has violated the usual male sense of decorum or decency. She celebrates a new age by doing so, an age seeking to forge new idiom, a new medium and newer modes of address, constituting a total rejection of the conventional modes of poetic experience of the dominant culture. She has given an altogether new poetic awareness for Indian women poets to assert themselves forcefully and without fear.

Her medium is a passionate inflamed assertion of that being which has remained mute, suppressed and battered through nameless centuries. The medium she employs is not only lamentably lopsided, but shows an alarmingly improverished angle of critical outlook in Indian writings in English. Her language in her poems is seen as the expression of the pitiable plight of a defenceless woman who needs love, consideration and sympathy and desires for a loving husband, warmth and home.

The conventional modes in Indian English poetry have been unable to convey reality, rather they have only glossed it over. Kamala Das confronts reality in its most brutal and ugliest forms. Her poetic techniques and language coalesce with her mood and with her experiences' content. Her most notable strength lies in confronting the reality of her experiences which in poem after poem becomes symptomatic of the general suffering of countless women.

With Sappho-like ecstasy and clarity of expression, she sincerely lays bare her woman's heart when she says:

What I am able to give
Is only what your wife is qualified
To give.

We are all alike,
We women,
In our wrappings of hairless skin.
["Composition," *The Descendants*, p. 38]

Things that came from her pen were something new, as no woman writer had ever before written with such power and honesty. Her poetry constitutes not just a compelling expression of personal experiences and a forceful subjective voice; but more importantly, a phenomenon unlike any other in Indian English poetry. She is the first woman poet to crack the mould, and establish an attitude and viewpoint the Indian readers were quite unfamiliar with and unused to. What makes her unique and unfamiliar can be witnessed in the following lines:

I wore a shirt and my
Brother's trousers, cut my hair short and ignored
My womanliness
["An Introduction", *Summer in Calcutta*, p. 60]

What Kamala Das wrote was so unconventional so hurtingly new, so outrageously anti-traditional. What the general readers reacted to immediately was the bold and frank confessional tone she wrote and her use of broad imagery seeking to convey the hurts and humiliations she received in her personal life. It is true that personal voice is very strong in her, and of course, depiction of her personality in its stark nakedness has made all the difference.

The diction of Kamala Das is also marked by an alarming speed and swiftness. The poem, "The Child in the Factory" represents the fact in this connection :

Angry glow, that factory
Dies.
Half drunk with sleep,
And sick with lies, I obey,

I recognize,
I love
[*Summer in Calcutta*, p. 30]

Sometimes the poet uses the same word in different clauses of a sentence to achieve this objective. Thus, in "The Inheritance", she writes:

Oh God,
Blessed be your fair name, blessed be the religion
Purified in the unbeliever's blood, blessed be
Our sacred city, blessed be its incarnadined glory. . . .
[*The Old Playhouse and Other Poems*, p. 20]

She adopts the seal of repetition to suit her purpose and the velocity of her emotion. Here, we see that not only certain words and phrases have been repeated, but a whole set of prayerful expression.

In creating her own language, Kamala Das surpasses all the possible linguistic conventions. In effect, her "All mine, mine alone" in "An Introduction" is a very powerful assertive language and a violent formula of expressing the very heat and dust of her humiliation in being a sabotaged and relegated being in the world. It is interesting to note that all this heat and dust is directed towards the forceful sexual politics ingrained in our social and domestic conventions.

Kamala Das would fain expressing about herself without leaving any secrecy from her person. She would fain expressing anything she feels from the innermost chamber of her heart as her conceptual predicament. "Cawing" of crows and 'roaring' of lions are involuntary and instantaneous outcries of the occasions. Similarly, the human occasions in the volatile circumstances prompt such involuntary outcries in order to give vent to the pent-up repressed feelings and emotions. What the poet implies here is the fact that her poems are the proper outcries of the occasions which are irresistible. The pleasure and the pain of these "cries" are inseparably involved. The love of expression on the one hand, and the agony of the expressed on the other, ultimately contribute to the sad outcries, i.e. her poems. In this context, her poetry takes its life-blood from the British Romantics and the modern 'Confessionalists' who always insisted upon pain as the necessary spring-board of human expressions.

The "man-made" language has become unsuitable for most feminist writers when it comes to the relation of their indepth emotions and relegated feelings. It is in this context that a number of feminist writers, including Kamala Das, look for new words, phrases and sentences of their own to fit into their desired expressionistic attitudes. Sukhmani Roy puts her viewpoint in this connection as :

> Feminist writers and critics recognise language as a major tool of women's oppression and realise the necessity of reinventing or reshaping language in order to allow women an entry into the symbolic order. Feminist writers like Virginia Woolf and Mary Daly have long recognized the unsuitability of man-made language which either trivialises or altogether silences women.[6]

Kamala Das' "outcries" are on the central ground of the painful experience of being a woman. The dehumanization of woman as a being has inflicted enough pain and the same has strirred her sensitive psyche with a bigger magnitude. Her spiraling self, like an insect pinned on a wall, left only to writhe and wriggle in painfulness cannot be tolerated anymore; she has to articulate her anger, she has to find a way to expound her emotional wounds and injuries. Verbalization of this indignation in her has to violate the socially accepted language formulas; and what pricks her sensitive psyche is to be honest, and, therefore, it necessitates stretching of her

> two dimensional
> Nudity on sheets of weeklies, monthlies,
> Quarterlies, a sad sacrifice'.
> [Loud Posters - *The Old Playhouse and Other Poems* p. 47]

The utterly honest confessions of Kamala Das even though sometimes extreme, are, answerable to the colossal fame she receives as a wife and a poet. She is also a self conscious poet, and does not pretend to be ignorant about her unique position as a feminist mouthpiece. This uniqueness is shown vividly when she says that her poems are :

The speech of the mind
That is here and not there, a mind that sees and hears and
Is aware. Not the deaf, blind speech
Of trees in storm or of monsoon clouds or of rain or the
Incoherent mutterings of the blazing
Funeral pyre'.

["An Introduction", *The Old Playhouse and Other Poems*, p. 26]

Her cadence boomerangs in the form of repetition and the choice of her words is a self-introspection or self-inquiry. For this one may refer to her poem, "The Stone Age" :

Ask me, everybody, ask me
What he sees in me, ask me why he is called a lion,
A libertine, ask me the flavour of his
Mouth, ask me why his hands sway like a hooded snake
Before it clasps my pubis. Ask me why like
A great tree, felled, he slumps against my breast,
And sleep. Ask me why life is short and love is
Shorter still, ask me what is bliss and what its price.

[*The Old Playhouse and Other Poems*, p. 51]

In this passage, the phrase 'ask me' has been repeatedly used to give it more prominence and emphasis. It is a feminist device desiring it to be heard by one and all. Some of the poems in the same trend are : "Substitute", "Radha", "Composition" and "Drama". The following is taken out from "Drama":

It was soon my turn to be the
Tragedienne, to take vague steps
Black gowned, black veiled
And wail, and beat my breast
And speak of unrequited love.
I am wronged. I am wronged.
I am so wronged . . . .
[*Summer in Calcutta,* p. 62]

There is a vestigial sign of emotional ruin in her poetic diction; followed by the anathematisation of life's realities. This is from "Substitute":

It will be all right when I learn
To paint my mouth like a clown's
It will be all right if I put up my hair,
Stand near my husband to make a proud pair.
It will be all right if I join clubs
And first a little over telephone.
It will be all right, it will be all right
I am the type that endures.
It will be all right, it will be all right
It will be all right between the world and me
It will be all right if I don't remember
The last of the days together . . . .

[The Descendants, p.12]

"It will be all right" has been used here also again and again, even in the context where the intentions of the poetess are juxtaposed. But there could be no better poetic tool for her than this as she is highly sensitive and extremely emotional and one who has been leading a life of tension and restlessness; and, from whose mouth, scraps of feminist yearnings should be throated out.

The repetitive application of words, phrases and sentences makes Kamala Das' poetry truly musical and rhythmical. It was Hopkins who introduced the "sprung rhythm", a rhythm of common speech and of written prose, when rhythm is perceived in them. Explaining the matter to Dixon, Hopkins said:

> To speak shortly, it (sprung rhythm) consists of scanning by accents or stresses alone, without any account of the number of syllables, so that a foot may be one strong syllable, or it may be many light and one strong.[7]

There are some advantages in using sprung rhythm. As the poet would not be bound to a fixed number of syllables in every line, he can get nearer to the natural and sometimes more forcible rhythms of ordinary speech. And, not being bound to an underlying rhythm dictated by a pre-determined metre, the poet has far greater freedom to make the sound of his words and phrases enhance his logical meaning. Hopkins had stated that "Rhyme removed, much ethereal music leaps in the air." Kamala Das, who does not practise "rhyme" in her verse, is a living example of "much ethereal music." Even if she had used some metre, she had not gone beyond the 'terse style'. The technique she employs may be comparable to the "sprung rhythm" of Hopkins.

She employs the traditional technique of the first person or the omniscient narrator. Hers is a kind of abrupt style which suits her subject or themes. She also avoids the use of the quotation marks to denote direct speech as in the following passage:

> When Iqbal refused to come to their place for
> Sunday lunches her husband grew moody. You are
> a suspicious woman, he said one day without
> any cause. What is the matter with you, she
> asked him. Has anything gone wrong at the
> office? Why are you picking on me for nothing?
> ["Iqbal", *Padmavati, The Harlot and Other Stories,*
> p. 59]

This creates her writing all the more dramatic and unique. Indeed, Kamala Das can be credited with having succeeded in achieving the effect of verbal economy which is rare in Indo-English writings.

The early poetry of Kamala Das suffers from certain weaknesses of technique. The repeated occurrence of words, for instance, in the first volume shows her lack of confidence in verbal medium. In spite of the mature control of the device in subsequent volumes, it continues in the form of the repetition of sentence patterns. There is an excessive use of dots which also incapacitates her poetic expression in the early stage. These dots, used by her and also by others, generally suggest either a meditative pause, or the beginning of the next stage of thematic development, or the incompleteness of the experience communicated, or the end of the stanza unit. Let us observe the following passage on how she uses the dots in expressing the significance of her expression :

> Of what does the burning month
> Of sun, burning in today's
> Sky remind me . . . . . . oh, yes, his
> Mouth, and . . . . . . his limbs like pale and
> Carnivorous plants reaching
> Out for me, and the sad lie
> Of my unending lust.
> ["In Love", *The Old Playhouse and Others Poems*, p.15]

We don't exactly know what the excessive dots used by her mean. Whether they represent the poet's intensity of lust, a meditative pause or the sun's scorching heat is in a dilemma. There can be 'much ethereal music' in her rhyme-free verse. Keeping apart such poems as "A Hot Noon in Malabar", "Summer in Calcutta" and "Radha", where we witness a cadence born of repetition of words and phrases, her poetical pieces like "The Doubt", "Glass", "The Testing of the Sirens" and "Blood" give us a sumptuous feast of musical delight and harmony. Of these, "The Testing of the Sirens" contains the following moving lines:

> I
> Shut my eyes, but inside eyelids, there was

No more night, no more love, or peace, only
The white, white sun burning, burning, burning . . . .
Ah, why does love come to me like pain
Again and again and again ?

Here, she talks about an aching love which has tormented her like a burning fire and this is a feminist inquiry as to why she receives this kind of sensation repeatedly.

The "Glass" has the following lines:

A woman - voice
And a
Woman small. I do not bother
To tell: I've misplaced a father
Somewhere, and I look
For him now everywhere.
[*The Old Playhouse and Other Poems*, pp. 21-22]

This excerpt may be marked for its internal rhythm - "woman" in the middle of the first line becomes "woman" in the beginning of the third line. While the consonance of "bother" and "father" is so evident, the terms "somewhere" and "everywhere" have an arresting jingling sound born of internal rhythm. Kamala Das is masterly in arranging her words and expressions in a highly musical form. She does not delight in litting cadence alone, but also in producing hoars and grating sounds. Take the following as an instance:

You dribbled spittle into my mouth, you poured
Yourself into every nook and cranny, you embalmed
My poor lust with your bitter sweet-juices. You called
me wife,
I was taught to break saccharine into your tea and
To offer at the right moment the vitamins. Cowering
Beneath your monstrous ego I ate the magic loaf and
Became a dwarf.

[*The Old Playhouse and Other Poems*, p. 1]

The frequent use of "b", "d" and "t" sounds and so many harsh and difficult words is to be found herein. They come in the form of an explosion as they are voiced and voiceless plosives.

Another characteristics of Kamala Das' poetry is her befitting figures of speech. Her alliteration is rough and tough and breathes fire and fury at places. Her alliteration comes into view, for instance, in the following passage :

> Love - born,
> It is only
> Wise at times, to let sleep
> Make holes in memory . . . .
> . . .   .
> Arena,
> That silent sleep inside your sleep.
> ["Luminol", *The Old Playhouse and Other Poems*, p. 12]

Mrs. Das' verse does not, in the least, fall short of such alliterations in many of her passages and the same may be located in "An Introduction", "The Suicide", Substitute" "In Love", "Love", "Composition" and "The Stone Age".

The use of simile by Kamala Das is also highly skilful and excellent. In her poem, "Drama", she likens 'an angry sun' to 'a red, red lamp' while in "The Stone Age" she compares the sway of "his hand" to a hooded snake. The application of simile is also found in "Forest Fire". Mark the following:

> Of late I have begun to feel a hunger
> To take in with greed, like a forest-fire that
> Consumes, and, with each killing gains a wilder,
> Brighter charm, all that comes my way.
> [*The Old Playhouse and Other Poems*, p. 39]

Here, the ferocity of her 'hunger' is compared to that of 'a forest fire'. The poems "Nani", "Convicts", "Annette" and "Gino" also have beautiful similes in them.

As the feminist hunger of Kamala Das finds expression in the simile of "a forest fire", she also makes use of metaphor in her verse in a noticeable manner. The short poetic piece, "Annette", thus offers this fact in the following lines :

Annette,
At the hair dresser.
Pale fingers over mirror-fields
Reaping
That wheat brown hair.

[*The Descendants*, p. 18]

'Mirror-fields' and 'wheat brown hair' are impressingly powerful and touching metaphors. More touching in her metaphorical statement about love is found in her poem, "Substitute" given below :

After that love became a swivel-door,
When one went out, another came in.

[*The Descendants*, p. 13]

Here, 'Love' is made a swivel-door. A swivel-door receives frequent opening and closing from the one who enters it. Similarly, Kamala Das' love receives frequent change of lovers indicated by the opening and closing of the door. It is definitely a powerful metaphor to give vent to the poetess' bitter feminist sense of love-making as a woman and her strong sense of disgust associated with it.

From time to time, the diction used by this poetess tends to be aphoristic and maximatic. Analysis may be made to delve into the realm of aphorism and maxim abstracted from her poem, "Substitute" as follows:

Life is quite simple now –
Love, blackmail and sorrow.

[p. 12]

The cadence of her words rings deep accompanied by universal truths such as love, sorrow and blackmailing. What she declares in this poem is not without some ecclesiastical manouverings and the readers are made to take it as an aphorism. She speaks this as a woman should, and also shows the discontentment she receives as a woman in this life and the world around her.

Kamala Das' "Composition" is also equally aphoristic, especially in the passage given below:

The tragedy of life
is not death but growth,
the child growing into adult
and growing out of needs,
discovering
that the old have black-rimmed nails
and scalps that emanate
a sweet mouldy smell.

[*The Descendants*, p. 36]

The first two lines, 'The tragedy of life is not death but growth' are equally moving lines written in an air of aphorism.

The diction which Kamala Das employs is rarely suggestive, since it is mostly "expressive" in character. An 'expressive' language spares nothing for the fancy of the reader and speaks aloud all sentiments and thoughts in a hurried pace. But in a poem like the "Maggots" there is a tone of suggestiveness:

At sunset, on the river bank, Krishna
Loved her for the last time and let. . . .
That might in her husband's arms, Radha felt
So dead that he asked, what is wrong,
Do you mind my kisses, love? and she said,
No, not at all, but though, what is
It to the corpse if the maggots nip?

[*The Descendants*, p. 28]

What effect does a corpse have even if the maggots keep nipping it – is a foregone conclusion that Kamala Das feels nothing of her husband's physical love. This short piece effectively suggests that Radha who is none other than the poet herself, has lost her true, ideal love for ever, and so her husband's offer of physical love to her is nothing but the 'nipping of the maggots' on her lifeless body ('corpse'). The language of suggestiveness begins to work in Kamala Das' poetry whenever she takes up the myth of Radha-Krishna, and to play it up as a vigorous symbol of genuine love.

The verse of Kamala Das is filled with picturesque scenes and sensuousness. Her abundant use of imagery renders her verse to be more auditory and tactile. It produces sensory effects on the reader, and sometimes the reader wonders whether he is not in the midst of Keat's poetry. The concreteness and the sensuousness found in her may be marked from the following lines :

> . . . How well I can see him
> After a murder, conscientiously
> Tidy up the scene, wash
> The bloodstains under
> Faucet, bury the knife....
> And, what am I in sex who shuttles
> Obsessively from his
> Stabs to recovery
> On her small silent room ?
>
> ["The Doubt", *The Descendants*, p. 22]

The given passage here is that of a copulation and the scenes associating it afterwards. It describes an act of sex, and is full of eroticism and sensuality. Mrs Das' poems are not sans the sex-acts of the male and female. Another poem which is more erotic and more sensuous almost like keats' "The Love of St. Agnes" and Coleridge's "Christabel", is The Looking Glass" given hereunder :

> Getting a man to love you is easy
> Only be honest about your wants as
> woman. Stand nude before the glass with him

So that he sees himself the stronger one
And believes it so, and you so much more
Softer, younger, lovelier . . . Admit your
Admiration. Notice the perfection
Of his limbs, his eyes reddening under
Shower, the shy walk across the bathroom floor,
Dropping towels, and the jerky way he
Urinates.

[p. 31]

And further, she goes on saying :

. . . Gift him all,
Gift him what makes you woman, the scent of
Long hair, the musk of sweat, between the breasts,
The warm shock of menstrual blood, and your endless
Female hungers.

[*The Descendants*, p. 31]

The 'fond details' expressed by the poetess needs proper evaluation. Here, we haves seen as evidenced by the lines, that she has had an exasperating and a long experience of love and sex with her man; and this very fact keeps the readers spellbound unto the very last.

Kamala Das speaks of herself and the experiences she receives as a woman. The 'nudity' of man and woman who are standing before a mirror and of their feverish and 'reddening' love-pranks have added not only confession but also more resplendence to the voice of being a woman.

The diction of Kamala Das is essentially modern and surcharged with emotion, she also adopts a matching poetic technique to suit her purpose and the demand of our age. For the energetic and sweepy expression of her verse, she did not require the artificial and gaudy technique of the school of Pope nor did she need the languid air and the love-lorn language of the Romantics; she rather needed the immense freedom and flexibility of the Moderns like Ezra Pound, T.S.

Eliot, E.E. Cummings, the Sitwells Theodore Roethke, Robert Lowell, Sylvia Plath, and Anne Sexton. She, therefore, took resort to free verse or vers libre, which allowed her ample freedom of utterance in verse form, without letting the emotions slip off or their intensity slide off. In the words of Sapir, a linguistic philosopher, language is defined as follows :

> Language is a purely human and non-instinctive method of communicating ideas, emotions and desires by means of a system of voluntarily produced symbols. These symbols are in the first instance auditory and they are produced by the so-called organs of speech.[8]

Kamala Das, in order to express her desires, ideas and emotions, has adopted the use of vers libre. In poem after poem, she applies the same technique, the same poetic tool. "The Suicide", "The Seashore", "Substitute", "The Dance of the Eunuchs", "Composition", "Blood", "The Stone Age" etc. are found to be in the tradition of free verse. Her use of the free verse is conducive to the manifestation of her feminist intentions and yearnings, her restlessness as a sensitive woman moving into the male-dominated society, and in them she appears as a champion of woman's cause.

The following is a passage where we find her use of vers libre in its texture or structure :

> It was hot, so hot, before the eunuchs came
> To dance, wide skirts going round and round, cymbals
> Richly clashing, and anklets jingling, jingling,
> Jingling . . . ..
> ["The Dance of the Eunuch", *Summer in Calcutta*, p. 9]

Here, in this passage we see that within a space of three-four lines the poetess has spoken so many things or persons. The season described here is 'hot' summer, and the 'eunuchs' coming to dance, their skirts following their motions, their cymbals producing sweet sound, and their anklets jingling in their dance. This kind of description in varied details in such a small place is pertinent to our scientific age, a gift which is hardly witnessed in the previous eras. Therefore, we may also say that Kamala Das is a woman-poet who writes with the flavour of modernism.

Evidently, Kamala Das is not as great an innovator in English as G.M. Hopkins or E.E. Cummings was, but she has emotions arrested in glowing words and phrases and she has skill to turn out brilliant images and similes, and these are enough to qualify her as a genuine poet in English. She writes in the tradition of Wordsworthian line that poetry is the 'Spontaneous overflow of powerful feelings; it takes its origin from emotion recollected in tranquility.......' She does not take interest in introducing new things in the art of versification. The employment of her powerful feelings may be seen from one of her poems, "Without a Pause" presented under :

> This paper, so bridal-white, write of
> Life's purity of life's betrayals . . . .
> Write of the seed's first awareness, of
> Children's malice, of adult love, of
> Darkened rooms, where the old sit thinking,
> Filled with vaporous fear.
>
> [*Summer in Calcutta*, p. 50]

The above lines give us a wisp of speculation or a whiff of feeling that she would love writing on a 'bridal-white' paper about the betrayals she receives as a woman. The consciousness and the awareness of life, and the realities surrounding it cannot be shaken off; and so, she would fain singing about them and thinking of them. She is all set to undergo a powerful pondering of the vice and the virtue which she receives within the ambit of her milieu as a woman. She must, according to her, keep singing whatever life offers; of malice, of love, or of darkened rooms, etc, without any pause.

In *The Old Playhouse and Other Poems*, she has included two poems written in the experimental style of E.E. Cummings. Although blank verse is not the share of her cup, she tries her hand at prose poems occasionally. Some of the poems written in this trend are : "The Swamp" and "Sunset, Blue Bird". In the former, we have :

> I am the tainted bush the poisonous snakes retreat
> At three am while the other sleep I have no
> Name of my own and my past is a desolate
> Terrain where memory like tall trees grow to my
> Malabar home years ago on hot moons the devil
> Dancers came walking past the bright rice fields
> Behind them the pariahs reed wailed a long wall
> Rising from the heat like a ribbon of pain
>
> [p. 53]

and in the latter poem, "Sunset, Blue Bird" we get:

> . . . I was warned not to go near the king but
> I did go and believe me he was like a man
> He clutched me to his breast he said he loved
> Me and I was happy and thought he was
> Happy too..... after a year two yellow moons
> Waxed and waxed without a sign of blood and
> I told him lying on his lap i told him and
> Suddenly the sun set on that beautiful face
> His breath was heavy in my ear he said not a
> Word . . . .
>
> [p. 54]

These poems may be compared with one of the poems of Cummings, perhaps, the following :

> Next to of course god America I
> Love you land of the pilgrims and so forth oh
> Say can you see by the dawn's early my
> Country' tis of centuries come and go . . . .[9]

or, with the following passage:

> Since feeling is first
> Who pays any attention
> To the syntax of things
> Will never wholly kiss you . . . . .[10]

In addition to the frequently used running lines to be had in Mrs. Das' verse, we come across a few exceptions in the forms of couplets and quatrains. Her poem, "The Flag" in *Summer in Calcutta* is penned in this fashion. Let's observe the following:

> The orange stands for fire, for fire that eats
> Us all in the end . . . .
> The white stands for purity that we dream of and
> Never find
>
> [p. 21]

and also:

> But why cry ? or, why even gloat
> In solitude ? what does a woman lose
> or even gain from a love affair ?
> The passions' dying is not a death
> At all but a sleep.
>
> [*With Its Quiet Tongue*, p. 32]

The neat arrangement of ideas in two lines does not conform to the fact that Kamala Das uses the heroic couplets dexterously in the tradition of John Dryden or Alexander Pope. As she is not highly educated, she may not possibly be aware or know of the subtle nuances of a couplet, and we cannot deny that she does not follow the great masters in this regard.

Similarly, her arrangement of lines in four for a stanza, as seen in the above or in "Someone Else's Song" (*Summer in Calcutta*, p. 31), does not subscribe to the traditional practice as in P.B. Shelley's "To a Skylark" and also, her poem, "Three P.M" (*The Descendants*, p. 21).

Apparently, Kamala Das is not as great an innovator in English as G.M. Hopkins or E.E. Cummings was, but she has emotions caught in glowing words and phrases and expressions and she has also the skill to turn out brilliant images and similes, and these are enough points to qualify her as an authentic poet in English.

Kamala Das, as a poet, makes ample use of images and symbols. These images and symbols are focused on her hectic search for true love; and her personal predicament gets reflected on them. She is a poetess mainly of love and sex and of the body, and hence her diction is a celebration of these aspects.

Her work is a compelling account of the presence of her own self. She speaks out her own heart from her own premise. She is a daring writer who tries to redefine herself and also tries to liberate herself both as an Indian woman and a poet. She struggles to cope with her problems and dilemmas. She does not try to intellectualise or be didactic, nor does she attempt to spiritualise. She makes a discovery of her own selfhood and narrates her experience with energetic force and feelings. She believes in herself and hence she denounces the role of a masquerader and refuses to accept the limitations of her biology. Look at the free use of her poetic diction which might not be sans an impingement of decorum in the following:

> My grandmother cried:
> Darling, you must stop this bathing now.
> You are much too big to play
> naked in the pond.
>
> [*The Descendants*, p. 9]

The passage here is intended to unfold the frankness she possesses; and she does it without any deviation of forthrightness making her passions uninhibited. She is free in her behaviour and she expresses what she likes without worrying of what other people would think.

Kamala Das must also be viewed in the light of her feminine consciousness while assessing her language and poetic diction. She acquired a kind of 'feminine consciousness' under hostile circumstances from the society of her childhood days. There were so many repressive forces which tried to thwart her personality into fragmentation. But she did not stoop down to such vulgar emotionalities or repressive agencies. Instead, she moved forward to assert her unique individuality without any remorse.

As a poet, she is fully conscious of her creative faculties and potentialities, and thus, she tries to break the chains and restraints that she finds in her social milieu. She indulges in self-awareness, self-exposure and self-introspection in order to define her literary oeuvre. Her aim in doing this is not to bring about her pompous self-exposure; but self-discovery and self-examination. She draws up her own road-map by structuring self-exploration in order to search for her lost identity as a woman and as a poet. In a crowded world of men and women she finds herself in solitude sometimes, and the tone of her language is powerful in such poems as "The Freaks", "My Grandmother's House", "The Sunshine Cat", "A Hot Noon in Malabar", "The Invitation" and "The Looking Glass", wherein, she also describes the aches and agonies growing inside her and disturbing her.

The writings of Kamala Das also evolve mainly from her inner self which functions like a nucleus. An analysis of her work reveals that the woman persona in her represents her own life mutilated and self-tormented by both past and present and resulting in a deep sense of crisis. She feels exploited and cheated by the civilisation in which she belongs to and of which she is a part. Her family, community and civilisation expect her to play the role of a faithful wife and mother. But she has not much respect and enthusiasm for the culture besetting her, and which she thinks, is not favourable in the dispensation of her intentions. She, therefore, has to break some of the traditional canons framed by the pro-misogynistic texture.

In the poem, "The Suicide" we see how the poetess struggles to maintain her individuality and the problem of her identity. She feels that her personality is being eroded as evidenced by the following lines:

I must keep the right distance
Between me and high.
I must keep the distance
Between me and the low.
O sea, I am fed up
I want to be simple
I want to be loved
And if love is not to be had,
I want to be dead . . . ..

[*The Descendants*, p. 8]

She is seen here to play the part of a faithful wife which is obligatory. She is not allowed to choose her lot. It is some male who compels her to choose her roles. She is forced to act either as a slave or an idol. Never was she a person who chose her lot. She is fed up, grows nostalgic and has to trace her ancestry by going back to her Malabar house.

Kamala Das seems to find no way out of her tormented life and deciphers that there can be no easy solution. She, therefore, has to bear her own yoke and fight against the power of patriarchy. Her poem, "The Conflagration" belongs to the group of poems that has given voice to the woman's spirit of rebellion against male domination and ego. There is a desire to free herself from subjugation as shown below:

Woman, is this happiness, this lying buried
Beneath a man ? It's time again to come alive,
The world extends a lot beyond his six-foot frame.

[*The Descendants*, p. 26]

Dwelling on the same point, we may not fail to see how she protests against the male domination or the belittling or the dwarfing of the feminine identity. The poem, "The Old Playhouse" is worth rehighlighting in this regard:

Cowering
Beneath your monstrous ego, I ate the magic loaf and
Became a dwarf. I lost my will and reason, to all your

Questions I mumbled incoherent replies.

[*The Old Playhouse and Other Poems*, p. 1]

Her language is of rebellion and she continues her "rebellious attitude" in such poem as "The Proud One", Captive", The "Conflagration" and "Substitute". This revolt squeezed out from her own personality is also accompanied by psychological trauma, frustrations and tumultuous hardship. But, the only means for the attainment of this ideal is to be driving through this male dominated world and society. Though her rebellion and the struggle for identity is sometimes, hindered by the feeling of anxiety, alienation, meaninglessness, futility, acute sense of isolation and fragmented-self, she never gets bogged down by these negative passions. Instead, she keeps fighting these forces and comes out victorious shunning and overcoming them.

Kamala Das as a poet and a writer could be a persona non grata at times because of certain weaknesses of technique and stylistic propriety. However, she deserves appreciation in the highest degree because her language is without any sham or crookedness. It comes to the readers with the force of a typhoon, and her readers have no choice but to hear and listen to her open confession and frankness. Her diction consists of diverse moods of passionate longing for true love, sexual urge, agonizing guilt, nauseating disgusts and bitterness. Images of deep involvement in the physical act of love are followed by those of physical deterioration and rotting. Disgust, fatigue and sickness are also found in poems like "In Love", "The Old Playhouse" and "Gino". Hers is a medium touching all the factual pulses and vestiges of life.

Kamala Das has a lot of skills and ability. She has employed the technique of frequent change of situation. She possesses chameleonic characteristics to suit situational needs. She is a powerful and a versatile writer who extricates all her indepth feelings with her expressionistic devices. Sometimes, she makes us laugh and at other times, she makes us cry. Sometimes, she makes us happy and at other times, she makes us tiresome and fatigue by the power of her words and phrases. We see and experience all sorts of passions and emotions which are humane in terms of the interspersion of surprise, love, sex, disappointment, striptease, anger, pretension, envy, disillusionment, happiness and sorrow, etc.

Despite all the weak points found in Kamala Das, she is very much a unique writer among Indian women-writers. And although she rebels against the male-folks, and as a result of which she might not be acceptable to them for her acting and opposing in ways defiant of social approval, yet she is very much a poet of herself and to herself and writes in a style which is unprecedented in the entire Indian writings in English. Her diction is as free as herself combined with a forceful conversational style. And although she defies all restrictions of metre and rhythm just as she defies every pro-misogynist culture, yet, hers is a style never attempted before in the Indian Feminist Literary Writing. Her attempt reminds us of the greatest English Epic poet of the seventeenth century, John Milton (1608-74) who wrote the following lines:

> I thence
> Invoke thy aid to my advent'rous song,
> That with no middle flight intends to soar
> Above th' Aonian Mount, while it pursues
> Things unattempted yet in Prose or Rhyme.[11]

What Milton had stated here of an endeavour which was never attempted in Prose or Rhyme is also true in the case of Kamala Das. Before she emerged into the Indian Feminist Literary scene, nobody or no woman had dared to speak about her body or of sex in its stark nakedness. No woman had braved to exhibit man-woman relationship in a crytallised mood or transparency. Crystalisation of her diction brings about a uniqueness of her own personality in the form of an x-ray and she seems to be like an unreined female horse that travels anywhere she likes.

Kamala Das rises above the average women in using her language, sentences, phrases or words as far as frankness or openness is concerned. She employs a technique to make her diction acquire aesthetic heights travelling through the universality of man-woman relationship. She will be remembered as a rare gem whose contribution has given enough light on the question of self-exploration and self-introspection. She has a chameleonic technique that thrills and entices her audience; and the autobiographic formula she adopts, with her forceful medium, lends it all the more authenticity and genuineness.

NOTES AND REFERNECES

1. *Encarta Concise English Dictionary*, "Language, diction, technique and style" (London : Bloombury Publishing Plc.) pp. 399, 810, 1437 and 1483.
2. Kate Millet, *Sexual Politics* (London : Abacus, 1972), p. 25.
3. Kamala Das, My story (New Delhi : Sterling Publishers Pvt. Ltd., 1976), p. 144.
4. Iqbal Kaur, *Sexual Politics and Kamala Das* (New Delhi : Prestige Books, 1993), p. 138.
5. Shyamala A. Narayan, "A Note on My Story" in *Indian Women Novelist*, Set II, vol. I ed. R.K. Dhawan, (New Delhi: Prestige Books, 1993), p. 174.
6. Sukhmani Roy, "Daphne Marlatt's Salvage": in *Of Language and Culture in Postmodernism and Feminism, Canadian Contexts*, ed. Shirin Kudchedkar (Delhi: Pencraft International, 1995) p. 198.
7. Ramji Lall, "A Note on Sprung Rhythm", *Studies in Poets, Gerard Manley Hopkins* (New Delhi : Rama Brothers, Educational Publishers, 2000), p. 31.
8. S. Venkateswaran, *Principle of Teaching English* (New Delhi: Vikas Publishing House Pvt. Ltd., 1998), p. 20.
9. E.E. Cummings, *American Poetryof the Twentieth Century*, ed. Richard Gray (Cambridge: Cambridge University Press, 1976), p. 112.
10. *Ibid.*
11. John Milton, *Paradise Lost*, bk.1 (New Delhi : UBS Publishers and Distributors Pvt. Ltd., 2004), p. 5.

6

Conclusion

The life-story of Kamala Das is shaped by myriads of conflicts and controversies. But though she is beset by all such problems and hardships, she is able to resist them by her own, and can stoically stand against such forces and repress them. She is able to face and surmount these issues because of her undeflecting courage and bravery.

Her life is an odyssey from innocence to experience, ignorance to knowledge and youth to maturity. After her unending conflict between her and the society or, between her inner self and the outer world, she at last felt to be at home with herself. Her unceasing search for an ideal love ends up to be a "fond conceit"[1] like that of Coleridge's yearning for the lost youth, and finally, she turns for her Hope and Aspiration to Lord Krishna.

Her revelation of her own life-story in the form of her own autobiography is unique and unprecedented in the genre of Feminist Writings in Indian English Literature. Such an effort by an Indian woman without bypassing or belittling individual experiences, would help women map out a new world of female space. Indeed, the works of Kamala Das have influenced many feminist writers writing in the post-colonial period particularly in the context of India. Her effort to carve out a new world of female space is of immense viability taking into consideration the subaltern structures of family hierarchy, where the woman often occupied a position of prime importance. Such a role of the delineation of women's autobiography would be conducive in the restructuring and the modifying of the accepted norm of patriarchal discourse in our society today.

In the contemporary literary works, especially written by womenfolk, the feminine voice seems to claim for perfect freedom in personal matters, chiefly in relation to love and sex. Kamala Das, as an Indian woman, also raises her voice high so as to protest against the established order and tries to affirm her distinct identity breaking the traditional taboos of love and sex which is canoned by the power of patriarchy or the outcome of the age-old male dominated society.

Kamala Das, as a contemporary Indian writer, attempts to dismantle any pro-misogynistic psyche which would mar the true identity in a woman. It is with this purpose that she launches a scathing attack, vouchsafed by her undeflected spirit, to the power and authority of the phallus.

Her mention of the words like adultery, nymphomaniac and other excessive feminine inquisitions though might have sometimes intruded the antique ethos and established conventions, are intentionally done, to drive home in giving an x-ray result of her true identity and individuality. Her autobiography, *My Story* will serve as a blue print for those who would like to follow her footstep or those who are desirous to reveal their personalities bare and naked, while upholding their own authentic individualism.

She is pure, original and a powerful contemporary Indian writer. As a poet also she is quite conscious of her artistic design and purpose as well as her responsibility towards her vision. She diminishes male domination and exerts her rights independently at the cost of altering her religion. Kamala Das has now taken her pledge on Islam. Her transformation of religion is also a clear indication that she enjoys woman's identity and liberty.

What women could not speak before the male super-power in the past has undergone a change. These women can now raise their voice in expressing what they want and feel taking cue of the daringness and the boldness shown to them by Kamala Das. Her poems and her works are a vehicle to bring out the suppressed tension in the minds of women, who are not able to speak like her. Her use of the Krishna-Radha myth is also a clear symbol of her indomitable courage. Because it is through this metaphor that she makes herself exalted to the level of the "divine". She considers Lord Krishna as her mate who comes to her in myriad forms and to whom she says:

> In many shapes shall I surrender to His desire.
> I shall be fondled by him. I shall pass through
> all the pathways of this world, condemning none,
> understanding all and then become part of Him.
> Then for me there shall be no return journey . . . .
>
> [*My Story*, p. 197]

When Kamala Das is only a corporeal body, she has the valour to merge herself with Lord Krishna who is divine and ethereal. When she is only a human being of flesh and blood, she is fain to associate her sex-motif to a divine being like Lord Krishna and yet, it is done to show that she is a true feminist writer.

Most of the poems are explorations of the gender roles any Indian woman plays while mentioning her own roles – the embarrassment they involve, the resistance they provoke, the conflict they create and the pain they cause – are all brought out vividly. She is truly confessional and this confessional mode becomes a device to formalize the process of analysis and adjustment of the problems that crop up from arranged marriage at an early age. In fact, the writing of her own autobiography, *My Story* can also be taken as a yardstick of her defiance against early marriage or force marriage. It is in this work that she mentions all her frustrations, doubts and anxieties stemming out of her early marriage.

Kamala Das, as a confessional poet, does not limit her concern only for herself. She has the capacity to transcend the purely personal and embrace the non-personal and finally merge with it. In her poem, "The Flag" she depicts the futility of national pride when poverty and blood-shed sow misery among the multitude. She says:

> Poor flag, dear one,

Your pride is lost, it is time to leave the sky
And fall, fall and hide
Your shame beneath this blood-drenched Indian soil
And lie there and rot.

[Summer in Calcutta, p. 22]

This expresses her deep concern for the people outside the personal circle. Her quest for her own identity makes her to be a confessional poet, and in the process she expresses deep sympathy in the sufferings of others – be it about an old woman's "longing look" from behind the window bars, or be it about a bleeding brown comrade in Sri Lanka, her poems initiate or facilitate the fusion of her self with the surrounding. It would not be unworth, therefore, to say that Kamala Das presents her views based on the broader regions of humanism where life is taken into account not as mere birth, copulation and death.

In her effort to discover her own self, Kamala Das, unknowingly shook the norms of a male-dominated society. There had been almost no change made for hundreds of years under patriarchy before the emergence of Mrs. Das in the Indian literary scene. Though she has crossed some of the limits permitted for a lady in our society, she has properly given her feminine yearnings and curiosity in the proper perspectives. She says:

The tragedy of life
is not death but growth,
the child growing into adults
and growing out of needs,
discovering
that the old have black-rimmed nails
and scalps that emanate
a sweet, mouldy smell.

["Composition", *The Descendants*, p. 36]

What she means by "growth" is not the growth of a girl into adulthood or a woman alone. Her "growth" here, signifies the growth of a girl into a wife and mother giving sketchy coverage of the experiences in terms of isolation, turbulence and depression wrought by the phases of time of a married woman.

After entering into the statehood of a married woman, she starts searching for an ideal love. But very soon she realizes the futility of her search. She finds the remedy worse than the disease. For example, she turns to a group of lovers when she fails to find or receive love from her legal husband. But "they said each of/them, I do not love, I cannot love, it is not/In my nature to love, but I can be kind to you ...." What she needs is not kindness but love. They only toy with her physical body and do not fulfil her psychic needs.

The pain and the agony of not finding a true lover torments her and a sense of defeat oppresses her and she finds no way out of this limbo of sex and the vicissitudes of married life. She becomes aware of the fact that reliance on body cannot carry her far enough, or barge her to fulfil her ultimate desire; and begins to learn that it is rather a trap which prevents her from experiencing true love. She discovers that, after all, the pleasures body offers are of cloying and ephemeral nature. In this regard, the Keatsian remark on the difference between Art and Real Life may be quoted as follows:

> Happy Love !
> Forever warm and still to be enjoy'd,
> For ever panting and for ever young;
> All breathing human passion far above,
> That leaves a heart high-sorrowful and cloy'd,
> A burning forehead, and a parching tongue.[2]

In real life, human beings enjoy the pleasures of love fully and to the maximum, but the pleasures of love, when enjoyed in excess give rise to a feeling of intense disillusionment. The enjoyment of the pleasures of love in real life leaves Kamala Das also in a most feverish and fatigue condition. She comes to the realization that love which thrives and flourishes on body is bound to wither with it and the search for true love in a world of philanderers and casonovas is a futile exercise. So she surrenders totally to the mythical world of Krishna and Vrindavan to seek lasting love and fulfilment. In this context, she imagines herself as Radha and finds comfort in the arms of imaginary Krishna.

Furthermore, she can also experience absolute liberty from the rigid social code and the constraints of super ego in the presence of Krishna. Contrary to her husband's love which chains and confines her, Krishna promises total freedom and security.

Ammalu, the younger sister of her grandmother, who was also a poet, exerted a great influence on Kamala Das. This grandmother, who worshipped Lord Krishna wrote several poems in His praise. Though she was pretty and eligible, she remained a spinster until her death. She remained very faithful to Lord Krishna to such an extent that she would fain preserve her chastity or modesty for His cause. In her last poem she wrote, "My Chastity is my only gift to you, oh, Krishna...." Her writings seem to have influenced and motivated Kamala Das very much.

Taking cue from her grandmother, Kamala Das surrenders her hopes and aspirations to Lord Krishna. The haunting image of Krishna becomes inseparable. She remembers him on her bridal night and when she is pregnant and also while playing with her son. He appears to her in so many shapes and continues residing in her consciousness. ".... whose blue face is/A phantom-lotus on the waters of my dream".

It is against the background that one can appreciate the significance of her Krishna poems. Her poem, Ghanashyam flashes in the following:

> And each time my husband,
> His mouth bitter with sleep.
> Kisses, mumbling to me of love,
> But if he is you and I am you
> Who is loving who
> Who is the husk who is the kernel

Where is the body where is the soul ?
You come in strange forms
And your names are many.
["Ghanashyam", *Tonight This Savage Rite*, p. 19]

The above poem depicts very nicely the transformation that was wrought in her by her relentless search for love. She realises that her husband can never establish a rapport with her soul, because "And each time his lust was quientened/ And he turned his back on me...." What she seeks is a total merger in her lover. But since it is not possible in the actual world, she searches for Ghanashyam, the ideal lover. Dissolution of the individual self and the total identification is possible only with her mythical lover. This is clearly shown and illustrated by the poem, "Radha", where she depicts the ecstasy Radha experiences in Krishna's embrace. The poem is shown below:

Everything in me
Is melting, even the hardness at the core
O, Krishna, I am melting, melting, melting
Nothing remains but
You....
["Radha", *Tonight This savage Rite*, p. 23]

Critics opine that the treatment of Radha by Sarojini Naidu and Kamala Das goes with a slight difference. Sarojini Naidu's Radha is not anti-sexual, yet sex is not the primary concern in the Radha poems. But in Kamala Das sex implies a deep sense of intensified relationship which is not devotional, it is very much human in its concern and very much down to earth.

In the hunt for an ideal love, the experiences she receives are innumerable and sometimes incongruous. Suffering and humiliation are undoubtedly the dominating themes in her works taken up for discussion. She airs her views with a boldness unparalleled and she hopes that the society might change their attitude to those who suffer and are humiliated. Kamala Das is obviously a poet of the modern Indian woman's ambivalence, giving expression to it more openly and frankly than any other Indian woman poet. The horizon of her expression seems to have no limit in the depiction and the investigation of the self. She can be claimed as one of the boldest women writers in Indian English Literature.

When it comes to the deliberation and the discussion of the depiction of anatomical images, she is frank and has no inhibition. Her lyric is erotic and there is a sparkle of exotica. Her language is always overwhelming and energising.

The works of Kamala Das basically lie on the podium of sex experiences. She is frank enough to speak about her sex life freely. Her body, with its numerous centres all over, records the contents of her daily experience. Her body is her Malgudi as everything seems to centre around it. It is her greatest curiosity shop. Besides, it is also her most indispensable and sensitive instrument of judging her world or the world around her. She accumulates evidence through its responses and records them in her own non-conformist and uninhibited way. It traps all sensations, all songs, all shifts and all situations. It also responds to all 'hurts' and 'stabs' that love can offer.

Kamala Das' oeuvre is a qualified dissertation and documentation of her lived experiences. And these are the experiences she encounters in the odyssey of her life of unusual distinction. Whatever experiences she records in her poems are also all intimations of genuine isolation and turbulence and not of tranquillity, which many readers might expect to hear from her. Her poetry, on this count, has also achieved a certain degree of uniqueness.

Her chief contribution to modern Indian poetry is not only the stunning frankness she shows in every line she writes, but also in making public a vast fund of agonies and information regarding woman's plight and psychic experience that lay hidden for too long in the private female sector.

She squeezes out all the feminine failures and success in a woman and etches out in all caustic details in full public view. And on that account, she has become, according to some critics, a female Pope of the brave new woman who can look to her with reverence for inspiration, guidance and commitment.

Kamala Das, in most of the occasions, might have been seen as a crusader of sex. But we are aware that when sex has been consummated it leaves the person bored and fatigue. In the like manner, one might not take her for granted that she is an epitome of sex-intrigue for all the time.

The impression her poems create may reveal her endless quest for love and sex. But the reader should be a discerning judge to understand the posture she adopts. Behind the lines there lurks a figure with a glint of irony in her eyes.

Modern poets are in the habit of using irony. In their poetry, one finds that fair is foul and foul is fair. They say one thing and may mean another. Their appreciation may be ridicule and their ridicule, appreciation. All this means that an ironist is a conscious artist practising his art with circumspection and sometimes with ambiguity. Kamala Das has also used irony to suit her situations and sensibilities.

Kamala Das had tasted almost all the recipe of love and the fragments that love can offer in this life. Her search for ideal love is of an extremist's bearing because she even tried adultely which is antithetical to the modesty of not only to a Nair Woman but to every Indian woman. And, that she would have journeyed beyond this life for the realization of her ideal is presumable and perceptible. That she would have even stolen the boom from Apollo's Laurel Bower for achieving her end had Nature only permitted her is also a foregone assessment.

Whatever may be the case, a close reading of the whole corpus of Kamala Das' works reveal that her thought, style and tone have attracted a wider readership for their lyrical directness, immediacy, and quickness. She has in them all the female sensibility and the female desires with forcefulness and forthrightness. Through her works and especially through her poems she defines and redefines herself, her fluctuating moods, her amatory experiences in a world peopled by fond husband, lovers and flirtatious friends.

In conclusion one can easily see that Kamala Das is a modern, Indo-Anglian poet, who is highly sensitive and feminine. Her works are a vast repertoire of feminist longing, yearning, and idealism. She has aired the sufferings and the humiliations of the Indian womanfolk in the appropriate perspective. She has also voiced her views and speculations with a boldness unparalled. She is definitely a poet of the modern Indian woman's ambivalence, given expression without any hesitation, but with originality and authenticity.

Her contribution to Indian Literature basically shows that the female body can be celebrated to the fullest extent although it gets hurt and victimised by male domination, and for which she whole-heartedly resents. She has also vividly shown the insignificance of man's manoeuvrings by demonstrating her own struggles in the realization of his ideal. Kamala Das may or may not be serious about woman's emancipation from male domination, but as a poet and a writer she shows her seriousness and artistic craftsmanship concerned with her own identity as a woman. While exploring and introspecting her own identity, she has also explored the possibility of adapting the abilities of men poets to voice her own feminine grievances as a woman, wife, and a responsible mother. Indeed, she has broadened the horizon of women's psyche by delving deep into her own identity to give a new genre and a new awakening of post-colonial Indian writings in English.

NOTES AND REFERENCES

1. S.T. Coleridge, "Youth and Age". *An Anthology of English Prose and Poetry,* eds. Dr. W. Ibempishak Devi, K. Kalidas Singh, Dr. G.A. Ibopishak Sharma, Ng. Kesho Singh (New Delhi: Frank Bros. & Co. 2002) p. 110.

2. John Keats, *Ode on a Grecian Uran* ed. Ramji Lal (New Delhi : Rama Brothers, 2000), p. 127.

Bibliography

PRIMARY SOURCES

A. Poetical Works

Das, Kamala, *Summer in Calcutta*. New Delhi: Everest Press, 1965.

————, *The Descendent*. Calcutta, Writers Workshop, 1967.

————, *The Old Playhouse and Other Poems*. Mumbai: Orient Longman, 1973.

Das, Kamala and Pritish Nandy, *Tonight, This Savage Rite: The Love Poems of Kamala Das and Pritish Nandy*. New Delhi: Arnold Heinemann (India) Pvt. Ltd., 1979.

B. Novels & Short Stories

Das, Kamala, *Alphabet of Lust. New Delhi*: Orient Paperbacks, 1976.

———— A Doll for the Child Prostitute, in *Padmavati, the Harlot and Other Stories*. New Delhi : Sterling Paperbacks, 1992.

Non-Fiction

Das, Kamala, *My Story* (New Delhi: Sterling Publishers Pvt. Ltd., 1976).

SECONDARY SOURCES

(i) Books

Anthony B, Susan, *On Women's Right to Vote, World's Greatest Speeches*, ed. Rohan (New Delhi: Rohan Book Company, 2004).

Carden, Maren Lockwood, *The New Feminist Movement*. New York: Russel Sage Foundation, 1974.

Chitnis, Suma, Feminism: *Indian Ethos and Indian Convictions in Women in Indian Society,* ed. Rehanna Ghadially (New Delhi: Sage Publications, 2001).

"Feminism" in *Columbia Encyclopaedia, New Illustrated,* (New York: Rockville House Publishers, 1978).

Culler, Jonathan. *On Deconstruction: Theory and Criticism After Structuralism*. Ithaca: Cornell University Press, 1982.

Davis, Allen. *American Heroine: The Legend and Life of Jane Addams*. New York: Oxford University Press, 1973.

De Beauvoir, Simone, *The Second Sex* (New York : Penguin Books, 1984).

Dix, Carol. *D.H. Lawrence and Women*. London: The Mac Millan Press Ltd. 1980.

Donovan, Josephine. *Feminist Theory: The Intellectual Traditions of American Feminism*. New York: Frederick Unger Publishing Co., 1985.

Drabble, Margaret, ed. *Oxford Companion to English Literature*. Oxford : Oxford University Press, 1985.

DuBois, Ellen Carol. Elizabeth *Cady Stanton/Susan B. Anthony: Correspondence, Writings, Speeches*. New York : Shocken Books, 1981.

Eisenberg, Helene Lamoure. *The Theme of Demission in the Works of Simone de Beauvoir*, Ph.D. Dissertation, University of California, 1978.

Eisentein, Hester. *Contemporary Feminist Thoughts*. London : Unwin Paperbacks, 1984.

Harish, Ranjana, "My Story" in Jasbir Jain, ed. *Women's Writing: Text and Context,* Jaipur : Rawat Publications, 1996, p. 214.

James Version, *New King, Genesis, The Holy Bible,* ed. Thomas Nelson Madras: India Bible Literature, 1983.

Jensen, Joan M. "Disfranchisement is a Disgrace: Women and Politics in New Mexico 1990-1940", *New Mexico Women: Intercultural Perspective*, eds. Joan M.: Jensen and Darlis A. miller. Albuquerque : University of New Mexico Press, 1986.

———, "The Campaign for Women's Community Property Rights in New Mexico, 1940-1960". *New Mexico Women: Intercultural Perspectives*. Eds. Joan M. Jensen and Darlis A. Miller. Albuquerque : University of New Mexico Press, 1986, 333-356.

Johnson, Barbara. *Gender Theory and the Yale School. Rhetorie and Form: Deconstruction at Yale*. Eds. Robert Con Davis and Ronald Schleifer. Norman: University of Oklahoma Press, 1985.

———, *The Critical Difference*. Baltimore: The Johnsons Hopkins University Press, 1980.

Jones, Maldwyn A. *The Limits of Liberty: American History* 1607-1980. Oxford: Oxford University Press, 1983.

Kaufman, Polly Wetts. *Women Teacher on the Frontier*. New Haven, Conn: Yale University Press, 1984.

Kaur, Iqbal, "Protest Against Sexual Colonialism: Kamala Das' My Story, in Jasbir Jain ed. *Women's Writing, op. cit.*, p. 234.

Kazin, Alfred. "Oates". *Harper's* 243 (August 1971) : 81.

Kealey, Linda. *A Not Unreasonable Claim: Women and Reform in Canada, 1880's-1920's*. Toronto: Women's Educational Press, 1979.

Keller, Evelyn Fox. "Feminism and Science." *Signs* 7, 3 (Spring 1982).

_________. "Gender and Science." *Psychoanalysis and Contemporary Thought* 1 (1978): 415-20.

Kelly, John. *Women, History, Theory: The Essays of Joan Kelly*. Chicago: University of Chicago Press, 1984.

King, Bruce. *Modern Indian Poetry in English* (Delhi : Oxford University Press, 1987).

Klaiman, M.H. "Masculine Sacrality." *The Encyclopedia of Religion*. Vol. 9. London: MacMillan Publishing Co., 1987.

Kohli, Devindra *Kamala Das* (New Delhi : Arnold Heinemann, 1975).

Lacan, Jacques. *Ecrits*. Trans. Alan Sheridan. New York: W.W. Norton & Co., 1977.

Lal, P. Ed. *Modern Indian Poetry in English: An Anthology and a Credo*. Calcutta : Writers Workshop, 1969.

Lasswell, Harold D. "Impact of Psychoanalytic Thinking on the Social Sciences." *The State of the Social Sciences*, ed. Leonard D. White. Chicago: University of Chicago Press, 1956. 84-115.

Lawrence, D.H. *Women in Love*. Harmondsworth: Penguin Books, 1960.

Lerner, Gerda. "Placing Women in History: A 1975 Perspective. *Liberating Women's History*, ed. Berenice A. Carroll. Urbana: 1976.

_________. *The Majority Finds Its Past: Placing Women in History*. New York: Oxford University Press, 1979.

Lorde, Audre. *Sister Outsider*. Trumansberg, NY: The Crossing Press, 1984.

Mailer, Norman. *Advertisements for Myself*, London: Panther Books Ltd., 1968.

_________. *The Dear Park*. London: Panther Books Ltd., 1978.

Mailer, Norman. *The Naked and the Dead*. London: Granada Publishing, Reprinted 1979.

_________. *The Presidential Papers*. London: Panther Books Ltd., 1976.

McGilchrist, Ian. *Against Criticism*. London, 1982.

McCutchion, David. "Must Indian Poetry in English Always Follow England," *Critical Essay on Indian Writing in English*, ed. M.K. Naik *et al*. Dharwar : Karnatak University Press, 1972.

Melville, Margarita B., ed. *Twice a Minority. Mexican American Women*. St. Louis: C.V. Mosley, 1980.

Melwani, Murli Das. *Themes in Indo-Anglian Literature. Bareilly*: Prakash Book Depot, 1977.

Mickelson, Anne Z. *Reaching Out: Sensitivity and Order in Recent American Fiction by Women*. London: Scarerow Press, 1979.

Mill, John Stuart. *The Subjection of Women*. (First published 1869) 12th Printing. Cambridge: The M.I.T. Press, 1989.

Millet, Kate, *Sexual Politics* (London: Abacus, 1972).

_________. *Sexual Politics*. New York: Doubleday, 1970.

Mitchell, Juliet and Jacqueline Rose. *Feminine Sexuality: Jacques Lacan and the Ecole Brendienne*. New York: W.W. Norton and Co., 1982.

Mohan Prasad Chakradhar Prasad Singh, Hari. *Indian Poetry in English* (New Delhi: Sterling Publishers Pvt. Ltd., 1988), p. 36.

Mohanty, C.T. "Under Western Eyes: Feminist Scholarship and Colonial Discourses." in *Third World Women and the Politics of Feminism*, ed. C.T. Mohanty, Ann Russo and Lourdes Torres. Bloomington, Indiana University Press, 1991.

Moi, Toril. "Feminism, Post-Modernism, and Style: Recent Feminist Criticism in the United States." *Cultural Critique* 9 (Spring 1988).

_________. "Feminist Literary Criticism." *Modem Literary Theory*, eds. Ann Jefferson and David Robey. London: B.T. Batsford Ltd., 1986. 204-221.

_________. *Sexual/Textual Politics: Feminist Literary Theory*. London: Methuen, 1985.

Molvi, Z.F. "Kamala Das: Homeless in the City" in *Collected Essays in Kamala Das: A Critical Spectrum* ed. Rajeshwar Mittapalli and Pier Paolo Piciucco New Delhi : Atlantic Publishers and Distributors, 2001).

Morgan, Robin. *The Anatomy of Freedom : Feminism, Physics, and Global Politics*. New York: Doubleday, 1982.

Moses, Claire Goldberg. *French Feminism in the Nineteenth Century*. Albany: State University of New York, 1984.

Myres, Sandra L. *Westering Women and the Frontier Experience, 1800-1915*. Albuquerque: University of New Mexico Press, 1983.

Naik, M.K. *A History of Indian English Literature* (New Delhi: Sahitya Akademi, 1982).

Nandy, Pritish. "Introduction". *Indian Poetry in English Today*. New Delhi : Sterling Publishers, 1973.

Narasimhaiah, C.D. *The Swan and the Eagle*. Simla : Indian Institute of Advanced Studies, 1969.

Oates, Joyce Carol. "Updike's American Comedies." *Modern Fiction Studies 21*, 3 (Fall 1975).

_________. *A Garden of Earthly Delights*. Greenwich, Conn.: Fawcett Publications, 1966.

_________. *Do With Me What You Will*. New York: Vanguard Press, 1973.

_________. *Them*. Greenwich, Conn.: Fawcett Publication, 1969.

_________. Where Are You Going, Where You Been in: *Stories of Young American*. Greenwich, Conn.: Fawcett Press, 1974.

Offen, Karen. "Reply to Cott." *Signs* 15, 1 (Autumn 1989): 206-209.

P. Chavan, Sunanda. "The Moderns II : Kamala Das" in *A Study of Indian Women Poets in English, The Fair Voice* (New Delhi: Sterling Publishers Pvt. Ltd.).

————, R. ed. *Ten Twentieth-Century Indian Poets*. New Delhi: O.U.P., 1977; 2nd ed. 1980.

Patel, Gieve. "Review of Summer in Calcutta" in *Quest*, 47 (Oct.-Dec. 1965).

Patrik, Paula. *No Step Backward, Women and Family on the Rocky Mountain Frontier Helena, 1865-1900.* Helena: Montana Historical Society Press, 1987.

Patterson–Black, Sheryll. *Ethnic Life Agriculture and the North Platte Valley.* Crawford, Nebraska: Cottonwood Press, 1984.

Pierson, G.W., "The Frontier and American Institutions: A Criticism of the Turner Theory" in *Turner and the Sociology of the Frontier*, eds. Richard Hofstadter and S.M. Lipset. New York: Basic Books Inc., 1968.

Pillai, Mira. "Review of The Old Playhouse and Other Poems" in *The Indian P.E.N.* (Dec. 1973).

Poster, Mark. "Postmodernity and the Politics of Multiculturalism: The Lyotard-Habermass Debate Over Social Theory." *Modern Fiction Studies* 38, 3 (Autumn 1992).

Pratt, Annis V. "The New Feminist Criticism: Exploring the History of the New Space." *Beyond Intellectual Sexism*, ed. Joan L. Roberts. New York: David Mckay, 1976.

President's Report, 1892-1902, "A Historical Sketch." Quoted in *Beyond Separate Spheres*, ed. Rosalind Rosenberg. New Haven: Yale University Press, 1982.

Rabuzzi, Kathryn Allen. *The Sacred and the Feminine: Toward a Theology of Houseworth.* New York: Seabury, 1982.

Radford, Jean. *Norman Mailer: A Critical Study.* London: The MacMillan Press Ltd., 1975.

Radhakrishnan, S., *The Bhagavadgita.* London: Greorge Allen and Unwin Ltd., 1948.

Rahman, Anisur. *Expressive Form in the Poetry of Kamala Das,* New Delhi, Abhinav Publications, 1981.

Ram, Atma. *Interviews with Indian English Writers* (Calcutta: Writers Workshop, 1983), p. 81.

Ramachandran Nair, K.R., *The Poetry of Kamala Das* (New Delhi: Reliance Publishing House, 1993).

Rani Lall, Rama, "Rebellion and Escape : Kamala Das' My Story" in Jasbir Jain, ed. *Women Writing.*

Rao, Vimala. "Kamala Das – The Limits of Over-Exposure", *Contemporary Indo-English Verse,* Vol. I, ed. A.N. Dwivedi. Bareilly : Prakash Book Depot, 1983, pp. 87-96.

Richards, Janet Radcliffe. *The Sceptical Feminist: A Philosophical Enquiry.* London: Routledge & Kegan Paul, 1980.

Rosenberg, Rosalind. *Beyond Separate Spheres : Intellectual Roots of Modem Feminism.* New Haven: Yale University Press, 1982.

Rossi, Alice. "Women of Action: Frances Wright." *The Feminism Papers from Adams to de Beauvoir.* New York: Columbia University Press, 1973.

Ruether, Rosemary Redford. *New Woman; New Earth.* New York: Seabury, 1975.

Ruthven, K.K. *Feminist Literary Studies: An Introduction.* Cambridge: Cambridge University Press, 1984.

————, ed. *Modern Indo-Anglian Love Poetry.* Calcutta: Prayer Books, 1976.

Sanasam, Reena. *Kamala Das : A Study of Her Quest for Feminist Identity* (unpublished Ph.D. Thesis, Manipur University, 2000).

Sassure, Ferdinand de. 1915. *Course in General Linguistics.* Trans. Wade Baskin. New York: Philosophical Library, 1959.

Schlissel, Lillian. *Women's Diaries of the Westward Journey.* New York: Schocken, 1982.

Sharma, M.L. *Kamala Das.* Patiala : Directorate of Correspondence Courses, Punjabi Univ., 1979.

Shaw, Bernard. "Woman-Man in Petticoats." *Shaw, Platform and Pulpit,* ed. Dan H. Laurence. New York: Hill and Wang,1961.

Showalter, Elaine, ed. *The New Feminist Criticism: Essays on Women Literature and Theory*. New York: Pantheon Books, 1985.

———, *A Literature of Their Own: British Women Novelists from Bronte to Lessing*. Princeton: Princeton University Press, 1977.

———, *Women's Liberation and Literature*. New York: Harcourt, 1971.

Singh, Sushila, ed, *Feminism and Recent Fiction in English*. New Delhi: Prestige Books, 1991.

________. *Feminism Theory, Criticism, Analysis* (New Delhi: Pencraft International, 2004), p. 22.

________. *Jane Austen: Her Concept of Social Life*. New Delhi: S. Chand, 1981.

Sinha, Krishna Nandan. Ed. *Indian Writing in English*. New Delhi: Heritage Publishers, 1979.

Siva Ramkrishna, M. "Contemporary Indian Poetry in English: An Approach," *Opinion*, 4, No.1 (July 1974).

Sjoberg, Leif. "An Interview With, Joyce Carol Oates," *Contemporary Literature* XXII, 3 (Summer 1982).

Smith, Paul. *Discerning the Subject*, Minneapolis: University of Minnesota Press, 1988.

Spivak, Gayatri Chakravorty, *In Other Worlds: Essays in Cultural Politics*. New York: Methuen, 1987.

Stanton, Elizabeth Cady. *Eighty Years and, More, Reminiscences, 1815--1897*. (New York: T. Fischer Unwin, 1898) reprinted New York: Shocken Books, 1971.

Stefano, Carolyn. "Networking on the Frontier: The Colorado Women's Suffrage Movement, 1876-1893." *The Women's West*, eds, Susan Armitage and Elizabeth Jameson. Norman: University of Oklahoma Press, 1987, 265-76.

Storr, Richard J., *Harper's University: The Beginnings*. Chicago: University of Chicago Press, 1960.

Tevis, Yvonne Pacheco. "Feminism and the Mexican-American Woman." *UC MEXUS NEWS 28* (1991): 1-7.

The Encyclopedia Americana, vol. 12. Danbury, Conn.: Grolier, 1984.

Turner, Frederick Jackson, "The Significance of the Frontier in American History, 1893." *An American Primer*. ed. Daniel J. Boorstin. Paperback reprint. New York: The New American Library, 1985.

Tuttle, Lisa. *Encyclopedia of Feminism*. New York: Facts on File Publications, 1986.

University of Chicago Records, Minutes of the Meetings of the Board of Trustees, 19 February 1873. Old University of Chicago Papers, University of Chicago Archives. Quoted in Rosalind *Rosenburg, Beyond Separate Spheres*.

Usha, V.T. "Kamala Das : A Critical Spectrum" ed. in Rajeshwar Mittapalli and Pier Paolo Piciucco (New Delhi: Atlantic Publishers and Distributors, 2001).

US News and World Report. "Author Joyce Carol Oates on Adolescent America." (15 May 1978).

V.T. Usha. "One Women's Autography: Kamala Das' *My Story*" in *Collected Essays in Kamala Das, A Critical Spectrum*, ed. Rajeshwar Mittapalli and Pier Paolo Piciucco (New Delhi: Atlantic Publishers and Distributors, 2001).

Veblen, Thorstein, "The Barbarian Status of Women," *American Journal of Sociology* 4 (January 1899).

Verghese, C. Paul, *Essays on Indian Writing in English*. New Delhi: N.V. Publications, 1976.

Wagner, Linda W. *Critical Essay on Joyce Carol Oates*. Boston, Mass.: G.K. Hall & Co., 1979.

Waller, G.F. *Obsession and Transcendence in the Fiction of Joyce Carol Oates*. Baton Rouge & London: Loussiana State University Press, 1979.

Walsh, William. *Commonwealth Literature*. London: O.U.P. 1973.

Ward, Lester. "Our Better Halves," *Forum* 6 (November 1888): 275.

———, "Genius and Woman's Intuition." *Forum* 9 (June 1890).

———, *Pure Sociology*. New York: MacMillan Co., 1903.

White, Leonard D., ed. *The State of the Social Sciences*. Chicago: University of Chicago Press, 1956.

Williams, H.M. *Indo-Anglian Literature*. Madras: Orient-Longman Ltd., 1976.

Wolgast, Elizabeth, H. *Equality and Rights of Women*. Ithaca: Cornell. University Press, 1980.

Wollstonecraft, Mary. *Vindication of the Rights of Woman*. Reprinted Penguin Classics. London: Penguin Books Ltd., 1985.

Woody, Thomas. *A History of Women's Education in the United States*. New 'York: Science Press, 1929. (230-247).

Woolf, Virginia. *A Room of One's Own*. Reprinted Harvest/ HBJ edition. San Diego: Harcourt Brace Jovanovich Publishers, 1989.

———, *Three Guineas*. First Printed 1938. San Diego: Harcourt. Brace Jovanovich Publishers, 1966.

(ii) Journals

Bordo, Susan "Postmodern subject, postmodern bodies". *Feminist Studies* 18, 1 (Spring 1992) : 159-175.

Burwell, Rosemarie. "The Process of Individuation as Narrative Structure: Joyce Carol Oates 'Do with Me What You Will". *Critique* XVII (1975) : 525.

Candelaria, Cordelia. "La Malinche, Feminist Prototype". *Frontiers* 5, 2 (Summer 1980) : 1-6.

Coward, Rosalind. This Novel Changes Women's Lives: Are Women's Novels Feminist Novels". *Feminist Review* 5 (1980).

Das, Kamala, *My Instinct, My Guru, Indian Literature*. 139 (Sept-Oct., 1990).

Kaplan, Temma. "Female consciousness and Collective Action: The Case of Barcelona, 1910-1918". *Signs* 7, 3 (Spring 1982) : 545-566.

Kaufmann-Mccall, Dorothy. "Politics of Difference: The Women's Movement in France from May 1968 to Mitterand." *Signs* 9, 2 (Winter 1983).

Kristeva, Julia. "Women's Time." *Signs* 7, 1 (1981): 13-35.

Loeb, Catherine. "La Chicana: A Bibliographic Survey." *Frontiers* 5, 2 (1980): 59-74.

Marks, Elaine. "Women and Literature in France." *Signs* 3, 4 (1978).

Naik, M.K. "The Indianness of Indian Poetry in English," *Journal of Indian Writing in English*, 2, No. 1 (July 1973).

Nandy, Pritish. "Indian Poetry in English : The Dynamics of a New Sensibility," *Indian Literature* (March 1971).

Offen, Karen. "Defining Feminism: A Comparative Historical. Approach." *Signs* 14, 1 (Autumn 1988): 119-157.

Olsen, Tillie. *Silences*. New York: Dell, 1978.

Padhi, Bibhu Prasad. "The Parallel Voice: A Study of the New English Poetry in India", *Quest*, 98 (Nov.-Dec. 1978), 39-46.

Parthasarathy, R. "Whoring after English Gods", *Perspectives*, ed. S.P. Bhagat Bombay: Popular Prakashan, 1970.

Peeradina, Saleem. "Review of A Doll for the Child Prostitute" in *Times Weekly* (June 19, 1977), p. 10.

Pillai, Nita. "Review of Summer in Calcutta" in *Poetry India* (Jan.-March 1966), pp. 63-66.

Rao, Vepa. "Review of Alphabet of Lust" in *The Hindustan Times Weekly* (Sunday, July 17, 1977).

Raveendran, P.P., "Of Mask and Memories", *Indian Literature*, 155 (May-June 1993).

Ruddick, Sara. "Maternal Thinking," *Feminist Studies* 6, 2 (Summer 1980): 348.

Saha, Subhas C. "The Dance of the Eunuchs," *Insights*. Calcutta : Writers Workshop, 1972.

Saradhi, K.P. "Three Indo-Anglian Women Poets: Gauri Deshpande, Roshen Alkazi and Kamala Das." *The Journal of Indian Writing in English* (Jan. 1974).

Scharff, Virginia. "The Case for Domestic Feminism: Woman Suffrage in Wyoming." *Annals of Wyoming* 56, 2 (1984): 29-37.

Sex: Mindless Surrender or Humming Fiesta? *Femina*, 6 June 1995. p. 19.

Sharma, M.L."The Road to Brindavan: The Theme of Love in Kamala Das's Poetry," *Contemporary Indo-English Verse*, Vol. I, ed. A.N. Dwivedi, pp. 97-111.

Sissman, L.E. "The Whole Truth." *New Yorker* (6 December 1969): 241-242.

Spivak, Gayatri Chakravorty. "Acting Bits/Identity Talk". *Critical Inquiry* 18 (Summer 1992).

Srinath, C.N. "Contemporary Indian Poetry in English," *The Literary Criterion* (Summer 1968).

Srivastava, Narsingh, "Some Indian Women Poets in English," *Indian Literature*, XVIII (1975).

"Speech to the 1860 Anniversary of the American Anti-Slavery Society." *The Liberator* (18 May 1860).

Stoeltje, Beverly. "A Helpmate for Man Indeed: The Image of the Frontier Woman." *Journal of American Folklore* 88, 347 January- March 1975).

Suleri, Sara. "Women Skin Deep: Feminism and the Postcolonial Condition." *Critical Inquiry* 18 (Summer 1992): 756-769.

□□□